13 Days

of

Silence

13 Days of Silence

The Murder of Rylee James

A Mother's Account from the Ashes

Teri Busse

This book is based on real events and personal experiences. Certain names, identifying details, and timelines may have been altered to protect the privacy of individuals.

First Edition
Editing by Page Grey
Cover design by Teri Busse
Printed in the United States of America

I will always look for you in the

pink skies.

- Mommah

Table of Contents

Author's Note

This book is based on real events I have lived and witnessed.

It is not written as a linear reconstruction because grief, trauma, and memory are not linear. What follows reflects how events were experienced and understood in real time and how that understanding evolved as more information became available.

This is not written in a conventional journalistic style. By design, it reads as a memoir because that is what this experience was: lived, not reported.

All facts are presented as they were known or documented at the time. Where conclusions or interpretations are included, they are clearly my own.

Some names and identifying details may be omitted or adjusted where appropriate.

Certain conversations are reconstructed to the best of my recollection.

This is not an attempt to sensationalize or speculate. It is an account of what it is like to live through loss, to navigate a system that does not always feel centered on the victim, and to carry questions that were never fully answered.

This book does not resolve what happened; it bears witness to what remains.

— Teri Busse

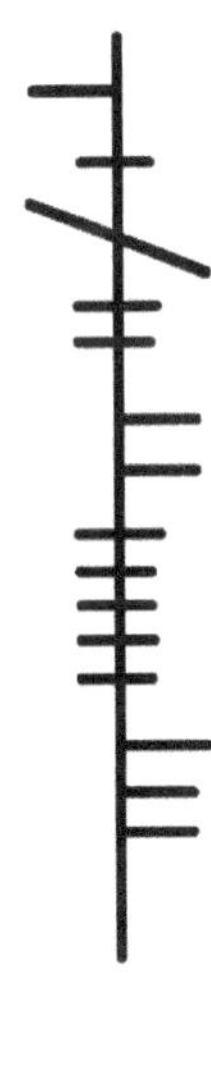

The Kindling

Chapter One

The First Lie

The first lie was not loud. It did not slam into me or ring alarm bells the way you would expect bad news to. It arrived quietly, concealed within a polite sentence from a man whose name I still do not remember. A detective, or a deputy, or an investigator. One of the many who would later blur together into badges, titles, and voices I could not separate, even in my sleep.

"We just need to talk to him; it's about a car," he said. "He is not in trouble."

Those were his exact words.

A car.

Not trouble.

Just a conversation.

I should have felt reassured. But the human body has its own language, and mine has lived in danger for twenty-five years as a medic. I know the tremor behind a calm voice. I can sense the shift in someone's breathing when they are leaving something out. I know when a sentence is too smooth, too pressed, or too prepared.

Something inside me, some instinct shaped by trauma and motherhood, addiction and survival, went cold as I listened to his words.

Something was wrong.

I did not know then that they already had my son's body.

I did not know that when that call came, Rylee had been dead for a day.

All I knew was that a stranger was telling me not to worry. Nothing was screaming. Nothing was obvious. Just a faint sense that something had been left unsaid.

People talk about intuition as though it is something mystical. When you are a mother, intuition is not magic. It is biology. It is memory. It is every scraped knee, every fever at two a.m., every "Mom, I'm fine" said with eyes that are not.

It is the animal part of you that recognizes silence where there should be noise.

Rylee never went silent.

Not with me.

Even during the messy years—the guns, the drugs, the bad decisions, the kind of life that stays two steps from disaster—he answered me. Maybe not paragraphs, but a thumbs-up, a "yeah," a "love you too." Something.

But that week in February, the messages stopped delivering.

Not "read."

Not "seen."

They simply stopped.

I refreshed the screen again and again, watching his name sit there, frozen in time, refusing to move.

Meanwhile, a different sequence had already begun.

The detective started asking the usual questions. Routine ones. Measured. But before he got far, I interrupted.

I asked directly. I remember my exact words were:

"Is Rylee okay?"

"Is he in trouble?"

I was told no. I was told this was just an investigation about a car. Not even his car, I was led to believe. Just a car. Nothing more.

That framing mattered. It was the difference between panic and patience, between pushing harder and trusting the process. I was being asked to stay calm, and I did because I was assured there was no reason not to.

But the questions that followed did not match the explanation.

When was the last time you talked to him? Does he have enemies? Has he disappeared before? Is he using? Does he own weapons? Who are his friends?

One question, in particular, stopped me. *Has he disappeared before?*

No one had said he disappeared. No one had said he was missing. If this was about a car, and if he wasn't in trouble, why was that even being asked?

That was the moment something shifted. Not panic. Not fear. Just the quiet understanding that this conversation was not designed for a mother. It was not reassurance. It was fact-finding.

It had always been about a car. But not in the innocent, wrong-place-wrong-time way I had convinced myself it was. Whatever they were actually investigating had started long before this conversation.

I was answering questions that no longer fit the story they gave me.

Not because I thought my son was dead.

But I no longer believed he was okay.

At the end of the call, he said it again, as if repetition could make it true.

"He is not in trouble. We just need to talk to him."

I hung up the phone before he could say more lies.

"You are lying," kept repeating in my head as I stood alone in my living room.

I stood there in transition.

There was a clear *before*, when the questions seemed ordinary and the explanation was almost believable.

Then there was the *after*. The moment I understood that whatever this was, it was no longer harmless.

I did not know yet what had happened.

I did not know where Rylee was.

I did not know how bad this was going to get.

But I knew this.

Whatever they were not telling me mattered.

And nothing would ever feel normal again.

Chapter Two

Before We Go Any Further

Before we go any further, there are a few things you need to know about me.

This is not an "About the Author" section. Nothing about this book is typical, and I'm not interested in pretending otherwise.

I am a retired paramedic with decades of experience in emergency medicine and am currently pursuing a doctorate in psychology. I have worked in emergency rooms. I have been a firefighter. I have been a corrections officer. These experiences form the framework I carry with me. This is where my observations come from, where my skepticism is shaped, and where my opinions are formed.

I am not writing from theory alone. I am writing from years spent inside systems that deal with crisis, trauma, and human behavior at their breaking points.

Early in my career, a field training officer drilled a simple rule into every report we wrote: "If it wasn't documented, it didn't happen."

That lesson stayed with me.

I understand how investigations work. I understand how institutions function under pressure. I know what evidence looks like when it exists and what its absence looks like.

Everything that follows is filtered through that lens.

I don't write in the way most people expect a true-crime book to be written or read. That's intentional. I don't enjoy reading long paragraphs myself; I lose focus. My brain skims. A wall of text makes me anxious, not immersed. I know I'm not alone in that, although it's rarely said out loud.

So I write the way I read. Minimal where it matters. Direct where it hurts. Detailed only when detail earns its place.

If something feels repetitive, it is. Not because I ran out of words, but because repetition is part of the truth. This is not the usual journalistic case review true crime book. When you get the same non-answers over and over, they begin to echo. The silence doesn't change shape; it only gets louder.

This book reflects that experience.

You will see the same phrases appear. The same explanations offered. The same gaps left unfilled. That is not lazy writing—it is documentation.

As a paramedic, documentation was my career. For twenty-five years, every call I ran either lived or died by what was written down. This is what it felt like to be told everything and nothing at the same time. *This* is true crime. There is no embellishment for comfort.

I also need you to know that I am not neutral. I am not objective. I am a mother writing about the murder of her son. Anyone who tells you that kind of loss can be filtered into clean detachment is lying to you or to themselves.

What I am is precise.

I worked in emergency medicine for decades. I understand timelines. Cause and effect. What happens when details are missed, and what it costs when they are. I know how systems are supposed to function, and I know what it looks like when they don't.

That lens matters here.

This book does not move quickly. It doesn't build toward a twist. It doesn't offer catharsis on schedule. It unfolds the way this actually unfolded—unevenly, quietly, and with long stretches where nothing happened except waiting.

If you're looking for resolution, this may frustrate you. If you're looking for honesty, stay.

Before we go any further, you need to understand how this story burns.

What happened did not begin with a fire. It began with the kindling. Small, ordinary things that didn't look dangerous on their own. Phone calls. Delays. Language that softened reality instead of naming it. Assumptions that bought time. Silence that felt procedural rather than intentional.

Kindling is what allows a fire to start without anyone noticing.

It's in the quiet buildup. They are moments that seem inconsequential until you realize they are not. This is where trust is formed. Where patience is rewarded with nothing. Where belief in systems is still intact.

Smoke is the first visible sign that something is wrong. Not fire. Not destruction. But just enough disturbance to make you pause.

Smoke Rising is when denial still feels reasonable. When explanations still sound plausible. When concern is present, but panic seems premature. It is the phase where questions begin to form, but answers are deferred. Where you sense danger without yet having proof of it.

This is where inconsistencies surface. Where timelines don't quite align. Where information arrives secondhand, incomplete, or delayed. Where you notice what is missing before you understand why it matters.

Smoke Rising is disorientation.

It is the period where instincts begin to speak, but systems still ask for patience. Where the smell is unmistakable, yet everyone assures you there is no fire. Where your body reacts before your mind is allowed to.

Nothing is officially wrong yet.

Nothing has been confirmed.

Nothing has been named.

But something is already burning.

Ignition comes later. That is the long silence. The months where nothing happens outwardly, but everything is already burning underneath. It's where waiting becomes a state of being. Where hope thins but does not disappear.

Inferno is the trial. It's the public part. The part people recognize as justice. It is loud. It is structured. It is exhausting.

And it is not the end.

The final section is what remains after the flames are gone. The embers. The ashes. The heat that lingers long after everyone else has walked away. The damage that doesn't announce itself but never fully cools.

These sections are not metaphorical. They are chronological. Emotional. Procedural. They reflect how this story unfolded in real life, not how it would be organized for comfort or clarity.

If you are looking for a clean arc, you won't find one. Fires don't resolve themselves neatly; they change form. They consume what they touch and leave evidence behind whether anyone is looking for it or not.

That is how this story moves.

Smoke Rising

Chapter Three

Thirty-Six Hours of Hope

The first hint that something was wrong did not come from law enforcement.

It came from Liz.

Liz was my old neighbor in Leavenworth. She is one of those people who become family quietly. A borrowed screwdriver here, a cup of sugar there. The kind of relationship where you don't need context before you return a call.

When her message came through asking me to call her, I did not think much of it. I do not even remember what I was doing when I saw it. I only remember that I called her back without hesitation.

She told me that the police had come to her door.

They were asking about Rylee.

They wanted to know if she knew him, if she knew where he was, and if she knew how to reach him. His last known address, they told her, was my old house. The one I had sold months earlier. He had not lived there in a long time, but they had to start somewhere, and starting meant knocking on Liz's door.

Looking back, that was the first time Rylee's name was spoken in a way that did not feel like my son.

It was procedural. Detached. Already in motion.

Not long after Liz's call, my phone rang. I missed the call. Then another. Both from Leavenworth County.

There was a voicemail. Polite. Calm. Nothing urgent in the tone. Just a request to call back when I had a moment.

No details. No alarm.

When I finally returned the call, the man introduced himself. A Detective, a deputy, an investigator. Over time, the titles blurred together.

He told me they were trying to track Rylee down.

"It's about a car we found," he said. "He's not in trouble."

I remember his words clearly because I asked him to repeat himself.

I remember my next words clearly.

I asked directly, "Is Rylee okay?"

Yes, he told me. As far as they knew, yes.

This was not an emergency. If it were, wouldn't it have been communicated differently?

I chose to believe him.

That choice was conscious.

I told myself that urgency has a sound, and this did not have it. I told myself that panic solves nothing, and calm had carried me through worse than this. I told myself that if my son were in danger, they would have said so.

When the call ended, life did not stop.

That was the cruelest part.

Nothing exploded. No second phone call came rushing in to correct the first. The house remained quiet. The clock kept moving. My daughters still needed breakfast. Socks. Backpacks. Rides. I still had to show up in my own life.

So, I did.

I went through the motions. I moved forward because nothing in front of me said I was not allowed to.

I did my due diligence. I messaged Rylee.

I chose my words carefully. I did not accuse. I did not ask questions that could pull him into something he did not want me involved in. I did not express fear. I kept it informative. Protective. The kind of message meant to alert, not to pressure.

The text I sent read:

Somehow, Leavenworth police got my number and are looking for you to "answer questions about a case." I told them I hadn't talked to you since Christmas and didn't know if you were in Missouri or Oklahoma. They asked if I knew an Ashley. I said she was an old girlfriend. I told them we do not talk but that I would give you the message. I also told them you do not have a phone and that I just message you. Anyways, I definitely don't expect you to call him, but I said I would message you. I just wanted you to know they're looking for you.

I sent the text with the number they gave me for Rylee to call.

He did not respond.

That alone did not frighten me.

Rylee had always been intentional about what parts of his life reached me. Not out of secrecy, but out of care. He understood the weight I already carried. Losing his stepdad had shattered our world. Helping his sisters through that loss had taken everything I had.

He knew that.

If he was caught in something complicated, he would have believed he was shielding me. That was who he was.

So I waited.

Hours passed. Then more.

The absence did not arrive as panic. It arrived as pressure. Quiet. Subtle. The kind that lives in the chest and does not announce itself until you realize you are holding your breath.

What unsettled me was not the silence; it was the combination of the silence and one of the questions asked by the detective.

During the call, he had asked the usual things. When was the last time I talked to him? Did he have enemies? Was he using? Did he own weapons? Who were his friends?

And then he further asked, "Has he disappeared before?"

That question did not fit.

Who said he had disappeared?

If this was about a car, if he was not in trouble, why would that question be necessary?

I replayed it later, not with alarm, but with curiosity. Like a puzzle piece from a different box.

Something about the conversation no longer felt tailored for a mother. It felt like fact-finding. Assessment. Information being gathered, not reassurance being offered.

I realized, without fully understanding why, that I had been spoken to as a source, not as a parent.

And it was only after I wrote this book that something dawned on me. When they asked me those questions, they either wanted me to confirm he was missing or to make me turn in my own son for a possible homicide.

I messaged Rylee again.

This time, I let the truth in.

I told him I was worried. Not frantic. Not accusing. Just honest in the way a mother can be when she is trying not to scare her child. Or confirm my own fear I was pretending did not exist. I told him I did not know what was going on, and that I did not need to. I told him I was not asking for explanations or details.

I just needed to know that he was okay.

One word would have been enough. A thumbs-up. Anything. Something that told me he was still on the other end of the silence.

Nothing came.

No reply. No acknowledgment. No sign that the message had even landed.

I stared at my phone longer than I want to admit, willing it to change. Willing his name to move. Willing the space between us to close.

It didn't.

The brotherhood of the badge still carried weight with me, and in that moment, I let it. Years of standing on the other side of the radio, of trusting procedure, hierarchy and intent, had taught me to believe that if something were truly wrong, they would say so.

So I believed them.

I trusted the reassurance. I trusted the calm tone. I trusted that if my son were in danger, urgency would have found its way into the conversation.

It hadn't.

That was enough to keep me still.

Not because everything made sense, but because I needed it too. Because the alternative required escalation, and escalation requires acknowledgement that *something* is wrong. Nothing I had been told gave me that acknowledgment.

But something had shifted.

There was now a *before* and an *after*.

Before, this was just about a car.

After, I could not say exactly what it was about, only that it was no longer simple.

I did not know what had happened.

I did not know where my son was.

I only knew that something no longer lined up, and that the space between what I was told and what I felt had begun to widen.

That was the moment the waiting began.

And before I could survive what came
next, I would need to remember who my son
was.

Chapter Four

Ry Guy

Rylee James.

I didn't choose the spelling just to be different, though I liked knowing no airport kiosk would ever reduce him to a standard Riley. I chose it because he was never meant to be standard.

Lee was my mother's middle name; James was my father's.

He was named after the two most influential people in my life: the woman who taught me tenderness and the man who taught me strength. Rylee James was a legacy before he was ever a headline. Before anyone else claimed his story, his name already belonged to something steady and rooted.

He was built from love before he was defined by loss.

Long before he was Rylee James in police reports and court documents, before his name was spoken by strangers who never knew him, he was Ry Guy.

That was what I called him when he was little. He was Ry Guy when he laughed so hard that he could not catch his breath. Ry Guy when he was proud of himself. Ry Guy in the quiet moments that belonged only to us. It was a name rooted in closeness, not correction.

When he was in trouble, he was not Ry Guy.

When lines were crossed, when he knew better and did it anyway, and when the tone needed to shift, he was Rylee James.

He knew the difference. So, did I.

But when he was hurt, or sad, or anything other than Rylee, he was Bubba.

That name lived in a softer place.

Bubba was the version of him that did not need words. The one who wanted quiet. The one who wanted me close.

When he was little, he loved it when I would stroke his forehead, tracing the bridge of his nose with my finger until his breathing slowed and sleep took over. That small, repetitive motion became our language. A promise. A way of saying I am here. You are safe. You can rest.

Sometimes I would sing "You Are My Sunshine," but I never sang it the way it was written. I would change the words without thinking.

You are my Ry guy, my only Ry guy. You never know, Ry, how much Momma loves you...

And when I reached the last line, I would always sing it softer.

Please don't take my Ry guy away...

He never needed the song to be perfect. He just needed to hear my voice, steady and close, carrying him into sleep.

That never really left him.

Rylee was born in Montana and spent his first decade there, raised in wide spaces and long silences. He learned early how to be outside and how to move through the woods without announcing himself. He learned how to watch the weather shift before it arrived and how to notice what does not belong.

Much of that came from the time he spent with my dad. My dad believed children should know how to survive without being afraid of the world. They camped. They fished. They hunted. They learned how to pay attention. Not in a fearful way, but in a grounded one. Watch first. Act second. Respect what can hurt you.

Those lessons settled deeply.

They became instincts.

Inside our house, Rylee carried another role just as seriously.

He was a brother.

Before Sydney and Rylee were born, there were already two boys in the house: Jason and Nathan. They were my first husband's sons from before our marriage, but they became *my* boys in the ways that matter. They were not mine by blood, but they were my boys just the same. I will always be thankful to their "real" mom, Julie, for allowing me to be their "other" mother.

When Sydney arrived, she joined a house that already understood the rhythm of siblings. And when Rylee came along, he stepped into a family where older brothers already existed.

To Sydney, his big sister, Rylee was the annoying little brother at first. As a toddler, he could not say her name. Sydney became Ninny—she still is. The nickname stuck because love does not always arrive polished. Sometimes, it arrives clumsy and sincere, and it stays forever.

For twelve years, Rylee was the baby of the family. In those years, we had already weathered big changes. I had remarried, and we had moved to Kansas. Through it all, he held that position with pride and more than a little resistance. He was not eager to give it up.

Then his first little sister was born.

Something shifted.

Not in words, but in posture. In how he stood closer. In how his attention moved outward. He became a big brother without being told to be. He was protective, watchful, and serious in a way that surprised me.

When the youngest arrived and took over the role of baby of the family, his instinct only grew stronger. He learned quickly who needed shielding and who needed space. Who could handle the world and who needed someone between them and it.

That sense of responsibility did not come from instruction; it came from identity.

Part of that instinct was something he learned from me.

I was a paramedic his entire life. At first, I tried to shelter my kids from my job. I thought that was what good parents did. I kept stories vague. I softened edges. I avoided details. But trauma does not stay neatly contained. Over time, it bleeds into tone, into habits, into the way a house holds tension.

Rylee grew up adjacent to reality.

Sometimes, as a trauma patient himself during testing scenarios. Sometimes, overhearing shop talk while adults debriefed hard calls late at night. Sometimes, just watching the way I scanned rooms, parked vehicles, noticed exits, and trusted my gut.

He learned without being taught.

Between mountain lessons, sibling responsibility, and emergency medicine, Rylee developed a kind of situational awareness that could not be traced to one source. It was layered. Inherited. Absorbed.

By the time we moved to Kansas, that awareness was already a part of him.

The mountains became streets. Trails became alleys. Weather patterns became people.

The same awareness that once kept him safe outdoors followed him into cities like Tulsa and Kansas City. He read rooms the way he had once read terrain. He noticed exits. He clocked tension before voices rose.

He trusted his instincts when something felt off, even if he could not explain why.

It was not bravado. It was familiarity with risk.

Rylee played soccer and football, but wrestling was his passion. Wrestling made sense to him. Control. Balance. Reading your opponent. Knowing when to press and when to wait. Discipline is disguised as aggression.

As he got older, the cities got louder. The stakes got higher. The danger wore different clothes. Still, he adapted. Not because he thrived in chaos, but because paying attention had always been how he survived.

He was loyal to a fault.

That loyalty was always both his gift and his vulnerability.

He believed people when they said they were his friends. He believed shared history meant shared values. He believed proximity equaled protection. Biology was never what anchored him. Loyalty was.

In the end, his loyalty was what betrayed him.

Rylee was a Momma's boy, and he was proud of it. He called me "Mah!"

Not softly. Not casually. It always came out sharp and familiar, like a summons and a comfort all at once. Even when he was grown. Even when he pretended he did not need anyone.

Tom, my husband and Rylee's stepdad, was the man he was closest to. By the time Tom was killed in a motorcycle accident when Ry was sixteen, Rylee had already severed his relationship with his biological father. That role was gone. The absence did not need to be named. Rylee felt it. He never spoke about the devastation of watching his biological father choose another life, but as his mother, I knew it lived in him.

When he got a second chance at a father figure and lost that, too, he understood what absence costs. He did not want his sisters to grow up inside that same hollow space. So he stepped forward without being asked. He became protective in ways that did not seek credit or recognition, doing the best a brother could do.

Sometimes, I think he felt responsible for us. Not because I put that on him—I never did. But because love mixed with loss can turn into obligation without anyone naming it.

Six weeks before Tom died, Rylee was in a bad car accident.

He was thrown from the back of a truck and knocked unconscious longer than was safe. His ear was ground down from sliding across concrete. Road rash covered him like clothing.

His friend, the driver, called me in a panic. When he said there had been an accident, everything inside me dropped.

I was standing in line at a gas station, my son fighting for his life somewhere else, the calm of one world about to collide with the chaos of another.

I arrived at the same time as the ambulance. My former coworkers looked uneasy when they saw me. They knew the rules. I knew the rules. No family in the back. I rode in back with him anyway.

He survived.

But something shifted.

When someone faces death that closely and lives, it changes them at a cellular level. For some, it humbles them. For others, it removes fear.

For Rylee, it was the latter.

After that, he lived louder. Faster. With a recklessness that looked like bravery on the outside and sounded like warning bells to a mother's heart. He believed he had already met death and was able to walk away.

Fearlessness has a way of opening doors that should stay closed. The kind of world where money comes fast and disappears just as quickly. Where loyalty shifts, and every decision carries weight whether you see it or not. It looks like freedom from the outside. It is anything but.

He moved through it like someone who no longer believed the worst could happen to him. Like he had already faced it once and walked away.

But even then, there were moments when something else broke through.

He talked about wanting something different. Welding school, "getting on papers," taking whatever consequences came, and going legitimate. A life that didn't require watching your back every second.

He was not tired of living. He was tired of living inside something he had already begun to outgrow.

In the weeks before his murder, we talked about it more than once. We looked up local welding schools together. I sent him the records he needed. He was starting to think in terms of a future that looked different from the life he had been in.

Still, underneath everything, he was Ry Guy.

This chapter exists because, without it, nothing that follows makes sense.

Without the mountains. Without my father. Without emergency medicine. Without siblings, love, loyalty, and instinct. Everything risks becoming a case file instead of a life.

He was never just evidence. He was never just a headline.

He was my Ry Guy. And he always will be.

As I was proofreading this chapter, it almost felt too short. Something must be missing. As if there should have been more time, more stories, more proof of who he was.

And then I was reminded why it felt that way.

At the age of twenty-one, they took my Ry Guy away.

Chapter Five

Thirteen Days

Time stopped behaving the way it was supposed to.

Days did not pass cleanly from morning to night. They folded in on themselves. I would wake up in that brief, suspended moment before reality returned, wishing it could last just a little longer. Then it would hit, and I would reach for my phone, refreshing my last messages with Rylee, even though I already knew nothing would change.

Silence became something physical. It took up space. It pressed against my chest. It followed me from room to room.

Waiting did not look dramatic. There were no sirens. No constant updates. No escalation that made sense in real time. What existed instead was absence. And absence stretched.

Information did not come from the places it should have. It arrived sideways: through

people, through rumor, and through fragments
that reached me before anything official ever
did.

A burned car.

A body.

No name.

No confirmation.

I don't remember exactly when I first
heard those fragments, and I don't think that
matters. What matters is what happened inside
me when I did.

My mind split.

Not gradually. Not gently. It split into two
clean, brutal possibilities:

Either my son was the body.

Or my son had put the body there.

Those were the only options.

If he were the body, hope did not
disappear—it hardened. I wanted it to have
been fast. I wanted him not to have suffered. I

wanted him not to have known what was coming.

If he had put the body there, then he was *still* alive. If he were alive, there was still something I could do. I could find him. I could get him a lawyer. I could help him untangle whatever had gone wrong. We could still survive it.

There was no third version. No misunderstanding. No version where everything was fine.

Waiting reduces the world to what you can live with. Alive, even if in trouble, felt survivable. Dead only felt survivable if it had been quick.

In my line of work, I knew what that meant. I knew the difference between death before the fire and death that comes from it. That is the moment you find yourself praying your child was shot and killed. Quick. Fast.

Your best case. Your new reality. I knew what happens when someone is trapped and does not make it out.

My mind did not stay general. It went to specifics: dents from kicking and punching, scratches that look like claw marks. Primal. Panic. Fear. The shape a body takes when it has fought and lost.

Those were not thoughts I chose. They were the ones that *would not* leave me.

I lived inside both realities at once.

From the outside, I looked fine. That was the part people misunderstood.

I still got up every morning. I made breakfast. I packed lunches. I braided hair. I answered questions in full sentences. I showed up where I was expected. My voice stayed steady. My face stayed neutral. My body knew how to function through a crisis. It always had.

I had learned long ago how to compartmentalize. I learned how to carry unbearable things without letting them spill outward. I treated those days the way I had treated scenes in the field. Stay calm. Stay useful. Do not fall apart where people can see you.

I was six months sober when my son was murdered.

There was no dramatic internal debate about whether I would drink. I knew what alcohol would offer and what it would cost. I made a conscious decision to stay sober and left it at that. I did not need to give grief one more thing to take.

So, I stayed upright.

I stayed contained.

I stayed sober.

Inside, I was unraveling in slow motion. I slept without resting. I ate without tasting. I smiled when I was supposed to. I measured every reaction. I edited myself constantly. I did not cry. Not because I did not want to, but because my body would not allow it. Shock does not always come with tears; sometimes it comes with containment.

The calls from law enforcement were few and far between. When they did come, they carried no urgency and no clarity. At the time, I still believed in the system. I understood investigations. I knew information would be withheld. I told myself the silence meant progress.

Meanwhile, the people who loved my son were not waiting.

His friends in Kansas, Missouri, and Oklahoma were already out looking. They were on the streets, asking questions, knocking on doors. They followed threads that were not being shared with me.

The contrast was impossible to ignore.

The people who loved him were searching everywhere. The people who were supposed to be looking were not calling.

Still, I waited.

Hope finds strange places to live. I told myself maybe he had turned his phone off on purpose. Maybe he was trying to negotiate his way out of something. He was smart. He had survived more than most people knew. I kept giving myself hope.

Then the request for dental records came.

Not confirmation.

Not identification.

Just a request.

You do not need dental records when someone is on the run. You do not need them when someone is being detained. You need them when there *is* a body, and confirmation requires proof.

Even then, hope twisted itself into something thin and desperate. Maybe the records would rule him *out*. Maybe it was not him.

I do not remember the exact day Amanda arrived. I only know that when she asked if there was anything she could do, I said no.

Amanda has been my best friend since my early twenties, long before Rylee was born. She knows me in a way that does not require explanation. She also knows I do not ask for help.

So she did not wait for me to.

She called from the airport. She was already in Ohio. She had flown from Montana because she knew I would never say yes if she asked.

She took up space with me. She sat in the quiet. She helped with the girls. She handled the practical things and the invisible things.

She did not try to fix anything. She just stayed.

Amanda was there when the second request for dental records came.

The second set was not asked for because the first had been misplaced. It was not paperwork. It was not administrative.

It was because the first comparison had not been enough.

There was no collapse. No screaming. No dramatic reaction. Amanda and I just made eye contact.

Good news did not survive a second request for dental records. Denial did not survive it either.

There was no speech preparing me. No softening of language. No gradual easing into the truth. Just the clinical mechanics of confirmation.

In the privacy of my mind, I hated what I thought next. In a frenzied last-ditch effort, I had hoped it was someone else's child. I hoped another mother would carry this instead of me. I hated myself for thinking it; I thought it anyway.

Hope does not require dignity; it only requires survival.

Three days later, while walking out the door to take Amanda back to the airport, the final thread snapped.

The confirmation came.

Not hysteria. Not panic. Just confirmation. Proof. Proof of what I already felt as a mother.

My son was dead.

The versions of reality I had been holding together dissolved without ceremony. The waiting ended. The silence shifted. The world did not explode. It simply narrowed.

Time did not move forward; it stopped.

Thirteen days had passed.

Nothing about time would ever feel normal again.

What came next would not be grief; it would be questions.

Chapter Six

The Celebrations of Life

I don't remember when it occurred to me that I would have to plan my son's funeral. Death creates questions. Funerals create lists. His obituary was added to the list of tasks to do. There was no dramatic realization, no collapse. It registered the way logistical truths do. Someone had to do it, and that someone was me.

There was no pause to grieve. No space to collapse. There were decisions to make. Flights to book. I had to fly to Sydney from Colorado. I had children to think about. There were phone calls that could not wait. I had to call Jason and Nathan and arrange their flights from Montana. I had to decide where my son would be honored while still struggling to say the word "*body*" without my chest tightening.

I knew there would be a gathering in Leavenworth. That was inevitable. It was where he evolved into a man. Where his life came together and unraveled at the same time. Where the people who loved him still lived.

A few days later, another truth became clear: there would need to be one in Montana too.

Montana raised him as much as anywhere did. The mountains that taught him awareness and survival. My family. My friends. The people who knew him before the streets complicated everything. There was too much history there to pretend it did not matter.

These would not be funerals; they would be celebrations of life. I held onto that distinction fiercely. I could not stand the thought of honoring my son in a place that felt heavy and final. I needed room to remember him alive.

Before any of that, there was the obituary.

Writing my son's obituary felt impossible. How do you condense one's life into a few paragraphs? How do you decide which version of your child the world gets to see?

Still, I wrote it. And when it ran, it was the first time his face appeared in print smiling. Not a headline about a burned car. Not a vague reference to violence. Just my son. An image of him *alive.* Human. Loved.

That mattered more than I can explain.

My memory of those days is fragmented. Entire sequences are missing. I have had to ask friends to help fill in the gaps. At times, that made me feel ashamed, like I had failed to witness my own life.

I know now that my brain was doing what it had to do to keep me standing.

Amanda flew in from Montana for the second time in a few short weeks. This time, Stacy came with her, another paramedic, another piece of home. I had known Stacy almost as long as Amanda.

Jaime came down from Topeka. I met her when I took my first EMS captain position in Missouri. She was a paramedic too.

I didn't ask any of them to come; they just showed up.

That's the difference between people who say they care and people who prove it.

They handled details I could not see clearly enough to manage. Food. Photos. Small things that somehow mattered enormously.

I picked up Rylee's ashes in Leavenworth.

Even writing that sentence still feels wrong.

The funeral home director was kind. He had also posted Rylee's obituary on their website. I could see my boy again smiling back at me.

Sydney, Amanda, and Stacy were with me when I went to pick him up. I remember sitting at a desk, though. I do not remember the words the director spoke. I am sure it was a speech he had given many times before. Different names. Different faces. Same cadence.

Then he handed me the bill.

Without missing a beat, I said, "Don't I get a discount? Most of the work was done for you."

With shock in his eyes, he replied, "Ma'am, it is a set price."

"MOM!" Sydney exclaimed, looking at me like I had a toaster for a head.

I apologized immediately and said I was kidding. Dark humor had always been my default. Amanda and Stacy understood. We had all been trained to function in the unbearable.

Still, the truth landed hard.

The last time I held my son, I was newly out of recovery. He was proud of me. He hugged me like he meant it. Now, he fits in a box.

Before I left, I took what will likely be the last photo of all my children together. Six of them. Sydney. Jason. Nathan. Lily. Sadie.

And Rylee, in a box.

His brothers were involved in every way they could be. They checked in constantly, asking for updates. They offered support without needing reassurance in return. That mattered more than they probably knew.

The Kansas gathering was overwhelming in ways I did not expect. People that I had not thought about in years showed up. Parents of boys Rylee grew up with. Those boys are now young men. Faces from every chapter of his life.

Later that day, one of the many faces from the past approached me and asked if she could speak with me privately. Of course, I said yes. We stepped away from the crowd, away from the eyes that seemed to be waiting for me to break.

She was nervous. I could see it in the way she hesitated before speaking. Then she asked if I knew what a *bruja* was.

I didn't.

She explained it loosely. A word sometimes translated as "witch," but not in the way people imagine. More intuitive. More seeing than doing.

She told me she had a vision.

She spoke without drama. Without embellishment. She said she saw Rylee burning. But then she continued, saying that she also saw Tom come down, take Rylee's hand, and lead him away.

Tom, the man who loved Rylee as his own, was there at the worst moment of his life. Tom was there, so Rylee would not be alone in this ultimate betrayal.

A father being there for his son.

I don't claim certainty about God, or spirits, or the afterlife. Grief rearranges belief. Some days, it strengthens it. Other days, it burns it to the ground.

I do know that something in me settled in that moment. If Tom had to die first to be there when Rylee crossed, then I could live with that. It was not closure. It was not an answer. But it made Tom's death feel less meaningless.

She will never know how much that moment mattered.

After Kansas, we went to Montana.

Sydney flew in from Colorado. The girls and I followed from Ohio. Jason and Nathan were already in Missoula.

I rented an Airbnb, not because no one offered to host us, but because I knew I would need space. I didn't know from what. I just knew.

I did not want my grief to overshadow my brother's recent wedding celebration. I did not want anyone to feel guilty for laughing in front of me. So, I removed myself.

My memory there is uneven too.

Amanda and Stacy organized most of the Montana celebration.

It was held outdoors, with the mountains stretched wide behind us. The same mountains that had taught Rylee how to survive. The same ones that had raised all of us in their quiet, stubborn way, steady, unmoved, weathering everything.

We gathered near the soccer fields where Rylee and Syd had spent countless hours playing, while I stood on the sidelines, always cheering them on. As I scanned the field, still images flickered in my mind: cleats cutting through grass, whistles in the wind, Rylee laughing after a goal. For a moment, I could almost see them moving again.

Looking at the mountains, I felt steady. Home. Grounded.

Looking at the field, I felt time folding in on itself.

Standing there, it all felt right and wrong at once.

Right, because this was home. Because this was where he had lived and run and grown strong. Because the people who loved him were here.

Wrong, because the reason I was standing there stood just behind me—a new shadow I hadn't asked for. The undertone of why we had gathered never left. It didn't need to speak. It was simply there. Close. Constant.

People stepped in quietly with food, framed photos, and decorations. No spectacle. Just love.

Amanda took the girls to gather wildflowers for the centerpieces, their small hands pulling color from the same ground where their brother had once run across.

It all felt right.

And it all felt wrong.

So many people showed up.

My EMS and law enforcement family came, along with seemingly every friendship I had made along the way. Even though I had moved across the country twelve years earlier. Time hadn't thinned the line between us. They were all there like no distance had ever existed.

Friends I hadn't seen in years came. Family stayed an extra day just to be there. Some of them, I would never see again.

But that day, they were there.

The stories carried me. At both gatherings, they did.

My boy was loved.

Not just by me.

I left Montana changed but not comforted.

I was sad. Solemn. Numb in a way that felt earned. There were still no answers waiting for me. No clarity. No justice. Just the long aftermath of loss settling into my bones.

But I had seen it. Over and over again. In the faces of people who showed up. In the stories they told. In the way his name moved through a room.

Rylee was loved.

Deeply. Fiercely. In ways I had not fully known while he was alive.

That knowledge did not fix anything. It did not make the grief lighter. But it gave it shape. It gave me something solid to hold when everything else felt hollow.

And under it all, beneath the flowers and the speeches, the laughter and tears, the hugs and shared disbelief, there was the thought that began in Kansas and has never left me.

When my son crossed, he was not alone.

Chapter Seven

Messages Sent and Received

People talk about family as if it is defined by blood alone. Parents. Siblings. Shared last names. But there is another kind of family that forms quietly, without ceremony and without obligation. It forms through loyalty, through shared history, through choosing to stay, when leaving would be easier.

Rylee had both.

There was the Rylee I raised, the one I knew intimately. And then, as he grew into a young man, there was the Rylee I knew about.

The version of my son who lived in a world I was never meant to be adjacent to.

That separation was intentional. It was his way of protecting me and his sisters.

We never spoke about it directly. We didn't need to. He knew I knew.

I voiced concern when it mattered. He heard it. He noted it. And then he continued on the path he had chosen.

It wasn't a secret that he was involved in selling cannabis. Legal in Tulsa. Illegal in Kansas and Missouri.

That difference created opportunity. It also came with risks he didn't want me or the girls anywhere near.

Once you live a life like that, you do not get to be one person. You become two: the version that belongs to family and the other that survives everywhere else.

In places like Kansas City and Tulsa, the line between ordinary life and dangerous choices can be thin. Rylee never would have told me if things were getting bad. Not because he did not trust me, but because he never wanted to add weight to a life he knew was already heavy. After his stepdad was killed, something in him changed. That was when he stopped burdening me with the things he carried. He never wanted his problems to become mine.

As his mother, I worried anyway. Always. That was the part he could not protect me from.

When he was murdered, people from his world stepped forward. Not loudly. Not for recognition. But because loyalty does not disappear when someone dies.

Ashlee

Ashlee had known Rylee since fifth grade. Long before adulthood had complicated everything. Long before choices began separating people into different versions of themselves.

It might have started with something small. Both of them carried conventional names spelled in unconventional ways, each ending in "lee." A coincidence that felt like recognition at that age. The kind that makes two kids notice each other and stay noticed.

Their relationship changed over time, as young relationships often do. But closeness remained, even when Rylee chose a path less traveled. They stayed connected not because of obligation, but because history mattered.

Ashlee was one of the first people I called during those initial thirty-six hours. She did not have answers. She did not pretend to.

What she did have was willingness. She asked around. She reached out. She listened. That was all I could have asked for.

In those early conversations, she shared pieces I hadn't known. Context. Fragments. Information that helped me understand the shape of my son's world outside of me. She had no reason to involve herself. No obligation to step into something this heavy. She did it anyway. Not because of the past, and not because of romance, but because she cared about Rylee. And because she cared about me.

Ashlee had known my son before any of this hardened. Before survival became a skill instead of a circumstance. What she offered was not speculation—it was memory. The kind of knowing that comes from growing up alongside someone, not circling them later.

That distinction mattered.

Because what I was beginning to understand was this: the people closest to Rylee were not guessing. They were remembering.

And they were paying attention.

Trevor

Trevor had known Rylee for years, not a lifetime like Ashlee, but long enough to matter. Long enough that his name came up often when Rylee talked about work. Construction jobs. Long days. Shared crews. He was a familiar presence in my son's stories, even if he was never part of my daily life.

To me, Trevor was a name. One that surfaced consistently. One that never raised concern. There were no alarms attached to it, no hesitation when I heard it. Just recognition.

Trevor was one of the few people I felt I could trust when the time came to make the calls. The ones I had been avoiding; the ones I hoped would bring answers. Not because I knew him well, but because Rylee did. Rylee trusted Trevor to be his person. And that made all the difference.

I later learned, not from the detectives, but through the way I learned most things in this case, that Trevor was one of the first calls made after the fire.

Rylee's car was registered to Trevor's address, making him an obvious point of contact. The calls came from homicide detectives, though that fact was not presented as significant when they reached out. Nothing about the call signaled crisis or finality. There was no disclosure of what had already happened. Just the same controlled framing. To me, it read as another example of omission, not an outright lie, but a withholding of context that mattered.

They told him the same thing they told me. It was about a car. Rylee was not in trouble. They just needed to talk to him.

There was no urgency in the tone. No indication that something catastrophic had already happened. No language that suggested danger or finality. Nothing that would have triggered alarm bells for someone who knew Rylee well.

That matters.

Trevor did not withhold information. He was not minimizing it. He was responding logically to what he had been told, filtered through years of knowing how Rylee lived. Rylee had laid low before. He had gone quiet when he needed to. Nothing about that call suggested this time was different.

Those initial conversations did not signal crisis. They did not sound like a search for a dead man. They sounded procedural. Neutral. Controlled.

So Trevor did not escalate.

Not because he did not care. Not because he did not think something could be wrong.

But because nothing about that call indicated that something already was.

This was Rylee. If he dipped, he would surface. That belief was not denial; it was precedent. And the detectives reinforced it.

Trevor filled in the blanks later. Not through investigation, but through memory. Through knowing how Rylee moved. Who he trusted. What made sense and what did not. He did not dramatize. He did not posture. He simply gave me what he had.

About a year after Rylee's death, I found out Trevor had named his child after my son. Later, I learned Cam had done the same.

That was when I understood the depth of their bond in way words don't fully reach.

Naming a child after someone is usually reserved for family, fathers, grandparents, bloodlines.

This was something else. Two young men, carrying him forward in the most permanent way they could.

That was not obligation.

That was love.

There are people who become part of a case because they are assigned to it.

And then there are people who become part of it because they refuse to stay silent.

Tina was the latter.

I didn't know her. She didn't know me. She found me on social media and reached out on February 28, 2022. It was before I had any definitive answers, before law enforcement had given me anything concrete at all. At that point, I was still living in uncertainty, still waiting for someone official to tell me what had happened to my son.

Tina had no obligation to contact me. She wasn't connected to the investigation. She wasn't asked to help. She wasn't looking for attention or proximity to tragedy. She reached out because her son had worked with Rylee. Because she knew him outside of this. She knew him as polite, kind, and memorable in the quiet way good kids often are. The way I raised him.

What she shared wasn't filtered through official channels. It wasn't curated or softened. It wasn't delivered in a conference room or wrapped in careful language. It was raw, unprompted, and real.

She provided Ring camera footage.

The motion-activated recording doesn't show faces—it doesn't need to. What it captures instead is movement in the dark, activity the camera can't fully register because it's night. And then, unmistakably, flames. Fire blooming where there shouldn't be any. Light where there was only darkness seconds before.

That is how the camera tells the truth.

What I am looking at in these images is not speculation. It is not interpretation. It is a time-stamped record of the moment my son's body was set on fire, captured not by investigators, but by a civilian's home security system.

I didn't receive this footage from the detectives. I didn't see it during the investigation. I didn't see it until after the trial.

I doubt I would know of its existence without Tina.

Tina was able to share it with me only later, when the legal constraints were finally lifted, when the system had already said it was finished.

Repeatedly, it was people like her, not the ones assigned to the case, who brought me closer to the truth. Neighbors. Strangers. Civilians who noticed something was wrong and refused to dismiss it.

The "silence" implied by this book's title isn't metaphorical. It's literal. For thirteen days, and for years after, some of the most meaningful pieces of information about my son's death came not from those responsible for investigating it, but from people who simply cared enough to act.

Tina wasn't family. What she did was refuse to stay silent. That gave us a bond that didn't need an explanation.

Over the two years between Rylee's death and the trial, she checked in, not out of morbid curiosity, not for attention, but as a mother whose heart was in the right place, who understood that something terrible had happened and that it mattered whether anyone was still paying attention.

In a process defined by absence, delay, and silence, Tina's refusal to look away matters more than she will ever know.

That is something I can't adequately thank her for. It is gratitude beyond words.

Cam

I finally met Cam in person in Kansas.

By then, I already knew his name. The same way I knew Trevor's. Not intimately, but consistently. Cam had been part of Rylee's world for years. His name had shown up in conversations about work and long days, and the kind of labor that leaves dirt under your nails no matter how hard you scrub. If I remember correctly, Cam ran a construction cleanup business, and the three of them worked together often. Cam, Trevor, and Rylee. A unit. Familiar. Steady.

One of my favorite pictures of Rylee comes from that time.

He had come by the house in a massive dump truck and wanted to give his little sisters a ride. The truck dwarfed everything around it. I have photos of the girls sitting one at a time on his lap, the steering wheel twice their size, huge smiles stretching across their faces. Rylee looks proud. Happy. Fully himself.

Moments like that are what make the other life easier to look away from.

At the celebration of life, those photos were on the memory board. When Cam saw them, he stopped and pointed, saying, "Hey, that's me." Behind me, I heard Trevor laugh and say, "Yeah, I was lying in the middle."

All three of them. Together.

Seeing that image and hearing that exchange landed differently than anything else that day. These were not just names I had heard through work stories. These were men who had been present in my son's ordinary life. The kind of presence that doesn't announce itself but shows up anyway.

That mattered more than I understood at the time.

Cam came to the hotel the day before the Celebration of Life. Until that moment, what I had was hearsay and speculation. Fragments passed along. Partial truths without anchors.

Meeting Cam changed everything I thought I knew. Until then, I had nothing concrete. No names that were connected to other names. No understanding of who knew who or how the pieces fit together. What I had was noise without structure.

Cam didn't arrive with theories. He arrived with receipts. Notes. Screenshots. Timelines. He walked into the room carrying a legal pad, not casually, not loosely tucked under his arm, but the way someone carries evidence when they don't trust anyone else to hold it. Pages filled front and back. Names. Dates. Arrows. Circles. Connections already drawn.

In one meeting, Cam gave me more clarity than Leavenworth County ever did. Not because he had authority, but because he cared enough to connect the dots. He looked tired. Not the kind of tiredness that comes from travel or lack of sleep, but the kind that settles into a person who has been carrying weight for too long. I didn't know the full extent of it then, but I would learn that from the moment Cam found out, he came back to Leavenworth and started doing what people in that world do when something goes wrong. Knocking on doors. Asking questions. Listening more than he talked. Pulling information from places I would never have known to look.

There are things I understood instantly and did not need explained. I did not ask how he got what he had, or why people spoke to him. I simply recognized the cost of it. Some truths don't need clarification; they only need to be acknowledged.

This was not grief scribbling. This was a man who had been doing something about what happened.

Cam was six feet two and carried himself in a way that immediately changed the air in the room. He didn't announce himself. He didn't fill the silence. He didn't soften his edges for comfort. His presence alone did something to people. The kind of presence that makes people uneasy without being able to explain why. The kind of presence that gives people who feel his presence a bad feeling.

I noticed it immediately. And I didn't regret it.

I had just lost my son. I did not need polite. I did not need reassurance. I needed someone who could stand in the dark without pretending it was light. Someone willing to look directly at things other people avoided.

Cam was that kind of man.

Rylee called him Big Homie. That alone told me everything.

Cam was older. Not by decades, but enough that authority didn't need to be negotiated. Enough that Rylee trusted him without posturing. Enough that when things started closing in, Cam was the one who Rylee reached for.

Cam had known my son for a long time. Back when I still lived in Leavenworth. Back when Rylee worked construction. Before Tulsa. Before Kansas City. Before everything fractured into separate lives and overlapping dangers.

These were not casual acquaintances. These were people Rylee trusted with his life.

And he did.

Cam didn't waste time showing me what he had gathered.

He started with the call log.

Rylee had tried to call him. Cam missed it because he was in the emergency room. He planned to call back. The first message he sent in response was a photo of himself in a hospital gown, telling Rylee he would call in the morning. At the time, the message sitting unread meant nothing. Only later did it come to mean everything.

When Cam told me this, he didn't dramatize it. He didn't justify it or try to soften it. He said it once, plainly. I could see the weight of it land in his body.

Guilt has a posture, and Cam carried it without spectacle.

Then he showed me the messages.

I took the phone from his hand and started scrolling. Down first. Then up. Rewinding time.

I saw the last message:

"bro shit all bad here."

Not dramatic. Not long. Not panicked in the way people expect fear to look.

Just blunt. Heavy. Final. A sentence that knows it might be the last one.

Just above the last message, Rylee had shared a Tupac clip from the movie *Juice*. It wasn't random. Cam recognized it instantly. In that scene, Bishop has crossed the line from friend to threat. The group is fractured. Loyalty has collapsed. Violence has replaced trust. Bishop believes he has power now, but what he really has is isolation. Everyone around him knows it, even if they haven't said it out loud yet.

The scene isn't about bravado—it's about realization. The moment you understand you are no longer surrounded by friends, but by people capable of turning on you. The moment when silence becomes dangerous, and trust becomes fatal.

Seeing that clip in the context of everything else changed how it read. It felt less like a quote and more like a signal.

Not a threat. Not performance. But an acknowledgment.

Something Rylee shared because he knew what he was standing inside of, even if he didn't yet understand where it would lead.

Twenty-four hours earlier, in this thread of messages, there was a photo of a gun. A description. A price. No explanation. No context. The lifestyle.

That part didn't shock me. I understood the world he had been navigating, even when I tried not to see it clearly.

But just above the gun photo, something stopped me cold: Rylee telling Cam he "*was done.*" Done with the bullshit. Ready to get on papers. Ready to be finished.

He had talked about it before: welding school, wanting something different. But seeing it there, placed where it was, changed the meaning.

This wasn't abstract hope.

This was recognition.

Things were closing in. And Rylee knew there was a narrowing window before getting out would not be as easy.

Cam showed me the GPS screenshots next. It was where Rylee was last pinged, when the location shut off. How it lined up with the time he was allegedly killed. He showed me photos of a house.

The house itself was easy to miss.

A small, tired rental tucked into a row of other forgettable structures. Beige siding faded unevenly by years of sun. Paint was worn thin in places, darker where hands had brushed past too many times. The kind of place that blended in by design.

The yard was neglected but not abandoned. Patchy grass. No flowers. No sign that anyone had ever tried to make it welcoming. The driveway was cracked and stained, with oil marks baked permanently into the concrete. Not recent. Not alarming. Just used.

There was nothing about the exterior that suggested violence. No tape. No visible damage. No indication that this address would matter to anyone beyond the people who came and went.

It looked temporary.

Not a home. Not a place you stayed because you wanted to. A place you stayed because it was there.

That was what unsettled me most. How ordinary it was. How easily it could have been dismissed as just another address. Just another stop.

Nothing about the outside prepared you for the weight of what happened there.

And nothing about it warned me that this would be the last place my son was alive.

The police had told me nothing.

Cam had everything.

At one point, I asked him what he would have done if he had answered that call. The question slipped out before I thought it through.

He tilted his head slightly, like the question itself didn't make sense.

Then his eyes answered.

He would have made his way to Rylee.

He had connections. He understood how these situations worked. He would have intervened.

That belief tore him apart.

Cam believed Rylee knew something was wrong in his final moments. That he knew he was being set up. What he didn't know, and could not have known, was exactly by who. That part was still muddy. Still unresolved. Still dangerous.

Cam brought what was left.

Not much. And that mattered.

Rylee lived light—he always had. A kind of nomad existence that never allowed for accumulation, only for choosing what was worth carrying. There were only a few things he held close enough to keep with him, no matter where he landed.

One of them was a large Alpha and Omega dedication from the Combat Veteran motorcycle club. It was big, heavy, impossible to ignore. It followed him everywhere. It wasn't décor. It was lineage. It was what he had left of the man who became his father. The man he called Dad. The man whose memorial tattoo Rylee carried on his own body. That piece represented belonging. Protection. Being claimed by someone who chose him and stood by him.

And then there was the Asics wrestling bag.

Black. Worn. Soft at the seams. It held the clothes he actually liked. The ones that felt like him. Not everything he owned. Just what mattered. That bag had been with him since middle school. Through moves, phrases, versions of himself that never stayed still for long. It was the closest thing he had to permanence.

When Cam set those things down, the room changed.

It wasn't dramatic. It was devastating in a quieter way. Visual proof that Rylee was gone, reduced to the few objects he had chosen to keep close. No excess. No evidence of a larger life left behind. Just identity. Just love. Just what he carried when everything else fell away.

Before Cam left, he did something that mattered more than almost anything else that weekend.

He gave me *permission*.

Permission to share his name. His number. His information with law enforcement.

This was not small. Cam was not someone who talked to police. Not without risk. Not without consequences. He carried a past. A world that did not welcome badges.

But because of loyalty, he was willing.

Because Rylee was family.

Watching him, I understood something essential about my son.

Biology was never what anchored him; loyalty was.

Rylee believed in his people. Trusted them. Stood by them. In the end, that loyalty became the very thing that betrayed him.

But in Cam, I saw the other side of it.

The kind of loyalty that keeps notes. Keeps timelines. Keeps knocking when others stop.

Cam did not save my son, but he did not abandon him.

And that matters.

This chapter exists because loyalty exists. Because without Ashlee, Trevor, and Cam, the story of Rylee's final days would be emptier. Easier to dismiss. Easier to reduce to rumor.

Cam saw him. Fought for him. Carried what was left.

And in a world where so many people looked away, that kind of loyalty deserves to be named.

There is something else that has to be said: Cam is now in prison.

Not for anything related to Rylee. Not for drugs. Not for violence connected to my son.

For something else entirely.

Something that does not intersect with Rylee's case but intersects sharply with the truth about this life.

I am not writing this to dismantle Cam. I am writing it because pretending people stay frozen in one moment is dishonest.

This lifestyle does not just take lives away. Sometimes, it corrodes people slowly. Sometimes, it pushes them into places they never imagined they would go. Sometimes, it strips away judgment, boundaries, and self-recognition until the line between who you were and what you've become disappears.

You can be the person holding the timeline. The one doing the work. The one trying to make something right.

And still end up reduced to an inmate number.

That's what people don't like to talk about. That proximity to darkness changes you. That surviving it doesn't mean you escape it. That even loyalty, even love, even intention do not grant immunity.

When your child has been murdered, you learn quickly that life doesn't divide cleanly into heroes and monsters. People can be both helpful and broken. Protective and dangerous. Loyal and lost.

Cam did not abandon my son.

That remains true.

And it is also true that this world consumes people in ways that don't always look the same. Some are buried. Some are imprisoned. Some carry the damage forward quietly.

This is not a defense. It is not an indictment.

It is a warning.

This life will take everything eventually. One way or another.

After everything I had been given by Ashlee, Trevor, Cam, and Tina—information gathered in the span of a single month, pieced together without authority, without access, without power—I held onto one belief: the police had more. I assumed they had to. If this much could be reconstructed by a concerned mother and kids, ones navigating grief and shock and loyalty, then surely, the people tasked with investigating my son's death were holding something deeper. Something clearer. Something that would eventually make sense of what I was seeing.

That belief is why I waited. Why I trusted. Why I gave them space I wouldn't have given to anyone else.

What never occurred to me then was that the truth might already be sitting in front of me, fully formed, and that the system would never catch up to it.

Looking back, that should have been the moment I understood. Not that the police were withholding the truth, but that they were never going to find it the way civilians already had. Through intimacy. Through persistence. Through caring.

The truth didn't arrive because of the system.

It arrived in spite of it.

The Ignition

Chapter Eight

The Long Silence

I did not call every day.

It feels important to say that out loud because people expect something else. Television has taught us what a grieving mother looks like. She is relentless. She calls constantly. She refuses to let the phone stop ringing. She demands answers. She is loud enough to be noticed.

That version of grief looks like love fighting back.

But real life is quieter than that.

I didn't call every day because I knew exactly how those calls went. I had spent decades on the other side of crisis, listening to people unravel, listening to anger and fear turn into something brittle once the adrenaline wore off. I knew the polite voices callers got. I knew the rehearsed empathy. I knew how urgency flattens when it's repeated too often, how concern turns into background noise when it isn't attached to something actionable.

And I knew myself.

Somewhere inside me lived a belief I didn't fully examine at the time. It was a strange, almost shameful version of *out of sight, out of mind*. Not because my son ever left my mind—he never did. He lived there constantly, even when I wasn't consciously thinking about him. But because calling every day felt like inviting answers that I already knew I would get. The runaround. The phrases. The calm deflections that sound like progress if you need them to.

I think, on some level, I believed restraint mattered. That patience signaled trust. If I didn't become *that mother*, the one who called too often, asked too much, demanded too loudly, the system would respond when it was ready. I think I believed there was a kind of dignity in waiting. That silence, if chosen, still counted as participation.

So I waited.

In the beginning, updates came only when I asked for them. Even then, they were sparse. Informal. They were almost entirely through text messages. Ninety-eight percent of our communication lived there—short lines, no tone, no connection. Nothing that felt anchored to my reality as a mother who had lost her son.

The language never changed much.

These things take time.

The case is active.

We haven't forgotten about him.

Those statements floated, unattached to detail, unattached to my questions. They were not lies, but they were not anchors either.

Life continued around the waiting. My daughters still needed me. They had already lost their father; they could not lose their mother to collapse or obsession or despair. I kept showing up. I stayed sober. I stayed upright. I did what I had always done in crisis—contained what I was carrying and kept moving.

Months passed.

Then, on Rylee's birthday, something shifted.

A friend called me. She was a mother too, and she didn't know the weight of the date when she dialed. But she understood the weight of what she was about to say. She told me she had learned that her child had knowledge. Not speculation, not rumor—knowledge. The kind that lands in your body before it reaches your mind. The kind that rearranges a room without moving anything in it.

This was not about my son being saved. He was already gone. We both knew that. This was about what comes after. About whether truth ever surfaces, about whether silence gets to be the final authority.

What mattered most in that moment wasn't the information itself. It was what it required of her.

She was not a distant witness, but a mother weighing her child's safety against another mother's loss. That calculation is not abstract, nor is it heroic. It is intimate and brutal. It is deeply human. It belongs to a world most people never have to enter.

We didn't decide anything quickly. We talked over days, not minutes. We named the risks honestly. These were not safe people. Violence had not stopped after Rylee was killed. Everyone involved understood what was at stake. There were no guarantees. Only consequences.

She did not owe me this. She did not owe my son this. And yet she stayed in the conversation. She carried the weight alongside me instead of handing it off.

When the decision was finally made, it was made deliberately. With eyes open. With fear acknowledged. With the understanding that once spoken, the information could not be taken back.

Only then did I pass it on.

That moment didn't feel like progress—it felt like trust.

Not the kind that comes from reassurance or rapport, but the kind that is extended anyway, cautiously, deliberately, because the alternative is doing nothing. It was trust that the police had not earned from me, and yet I was giving it fully. Not in pieces. Not conditionally. I gave them everything I had, and now it involved others.

There were no demands attached to it. No ultimatums. Just the expectation, unspoken but absolute, that this mattered. That my son mattered.

I believed that when something real was placed in their hands, when someone was willing to risk their own safety because they knew something, it would change the trajectory of what followed.

It did not.

There was no acceleration. No shift in tone. No indication that the weight of what had been offered registered in any meaningful way.

There was only silence.

Not the kind that signals strategy or careful movement. The kind that settles in once urgency has evaporated. The kind that stretches without explanation.

Months passed.

By the end of 2022, eleven months of investigation had already happened. I could count on one hand, with fingers still remaining, the number of times I had heard from detectives without initiating contact myself.

No updates. No check-ins. No indication that what had been handed to them had altered anything.

Nearly a year after my son was murdered, I reached out again. This time, I asked the question directly. I asked whether the case was going to go cold.

As with everything else, I left a message and waited for a call or text back.

The response came by email, which was new. It was dated January 23, 2023, confirming almost a year since the murder.

What I did not notice then but could not ignore now, when I later reviewed my records for this book, was who the email came from. The signature line no longer belonged to a *homicide* detective—it came from *narcotics*.

At the time, it meant nothing to me. Now, it explains almost everything.

It was professional. Measured. Calm in the way official language often is. And somehow colder for it. More impersonal.

I was told the investigation was still active. It would not be classified as a cold case. That the bulk of the work had been completed and would be presented to the County Attorney's Office for review.

I was told this process would take time.

I read it carefully—more than once.

There was nothing in it that suggested abandonment; nothing that told me to stop waiting. So I didn't.

Months passed again. No updates arrived unless I requested them. Nothing shifted. The language stayed the same. Reassuring without substance. Active without movement.

It would be easy now to say I should have known, and to say I should have pushed harder. Called more often. Demanded more. But that ignores what waiting actually does to a person. Waiting becomes its own logic. It teaches you to ration hope. Believing patience is still participation.

What I couldn't yet articulate, what I would only understand later, was that something fundamental felt misaligned. Not wrong exactly. Just off. The center of gravity never settled where I expected it to. The investigation was described as active, complete, ongoing, yet nothing about it felt anchored to my son.

I didn't name that yet—I couldn't—but in hindsight, oh, how I felt it.

By the time I stopped waiting and created the "Justice for Rylee" page in December of 2023, nearly two years had passed since my son was murdered. It was one year since the informal email that said "the bulk of the work had been completed and would be presented to the County Attorney's Office for review."

My decision didn't come from panic or impulse—it came from erosion. From the realization that waiting had become indistinguishable from standing still.

Whatever I had believed about patience protecting my son was no longer true.

Waiting had not brought answers.
Silence had not honored his life.

So I stopped waiting.

Chapter Nine

#Justiceforryleejames

This was not a whim.

Long before I created the "Justice for Rylee James" page, I had already been reaching outward quietly, carefully, to the people I trusted most. Not to the detectives assigned to my son's case. Not to the ones who barely spoke, whose silence had become familiar.

I reached out instead to two retired detectives who had known me long before I was a grieving mother.

JC was one of them.

I have known JC since middle school. By the time I entered the EMS world, he was already a paramedic. He was a mentor, whether he realized it or not. Later, he became a city police officer, then a detective. To say I trust JC feels unnecessary—of course, I do. That trust was built over decades, not conversations.

During the long stretches of silence in Rylee's case, I probably bothered him more than I'd like to admit with late-night text messages. The kind that come when the house is quiet and your mind won't shut off. He never once seemed bothered, not even when the questions circled back on themselves.

JC had never fed me false hope. He gave me hard truths when I needed them. Perspective when I was spiraling. Assurance without embellishment. Reality without cruelty. I know now that I made it through some of my darkest days because JC cared enough to keep responding.

The second person was Richard Hadar.

I met Hadar when I first got into EMS. Always going by his last name, he was a seasoned paramedic and highway patrol officer. Years later, he adopted a dog from me that needed to be rehomed, which is a roundabout way of saying that trust was already there.

Hadar had retired long ago and moved to a quiet, beautiful mountain landscape. But retirement didn't slow him down; it merely shifted him.

When my husband was killed in a motorcycle accident years earlier, the official conclusion was simple. An accident. No cause. No explanation. Just an ending.

If you've lived through that kind of loss, you understand how hollow that feels. "He crashed and died" may not be the exact wording, but it's how it lands.

Hadar reached out to me then and told me he had started an investigation company in his "retirement." He offered to gather the information, recreate what he could, and see if there was more than *nothing*. As generous as his offer was, I wasn't in a place to pursue it.

At the time, I had a seven-month-old and a three-year-old. Rylee was sixteen. Sydney had just turned eighteen. I had to be a mom.

But the gesture never left me.

So when my frustration with Rylee's investigation finally reached a breaking point, I reached out to Hadar.

Like JC, he had been following what was happening. He knew how little I had been given. I asked if he would look into Rylee's murder. Without hesitation, he said yes.

That conversation came from another middle-of-the-night message. Because nothing about murder lives between nine and five, no matter how much anyone pretends it does.

I sent him everything I had. Every screenshot. Every message. Every fragment. And without realizing it at the time, he took one of my darkest nightmares away.

Not through action, but through clarity.

After sending everything, I finally opened Rylee's death certificate, which had sat unopened for eighteen months. A seemingly benign piece of mail. But when it comes from Front Range Forensics, you know what's inside. I knew, because my husband's had arrived the same way years before. Quietly. Unceremoniously.

I opened it that day.

Manner of Death: Homicide.

Cause: Gunshot wound to the head. Thermal burns.

In that moment, for the first time, the image of my son being burned alive was no longer an option my mind had to entertain.

After giving Hadar the information, we talked. More accurately, he let me talk. Just like JC had. I was given a voice when I desperately needed one.

In a gesture that could never be thanked enough, Richard offered, along with his partner, to go to Leavenworth on their own dime. Not as friends trying to comfort me, but as private investigators who believed there were unanswered questions worth pressing. He understood what the absence of follow-up meant. He understood where cases stalled and why. His offer was not symbolic. It was practical, informed, and rooted in the belief that the answers did not simply vanish because the system stopped asking.

That kind of offer carries weight. It acknowledged, quietly and professionally, that what had been done was not the same as what had been finished.

What all of this did, without me realizing it at the time, was push me forward. Not into anger, but into action. No more passive waiting.

Three days after that conversation, after hearing plainly that I might be receiving far less than I deserved, I created the "Justice for Rylee James" page.

And three days after that, my phone rang.

Before we get into the phone call from the Leavenworth County District Attorney, I want to talk about the Facebook page.

#JusticeForRyleeJames was not created impulsively. It was deliberate. And the first deliberate choice I made was to *not* use my son's legal last name.

Whether people like to hear it or not, Rylee was estranged from his biological father. If you knew him, you understood why. It wasn't bitterness; it was lived experience. It was earned distance.

So, for my son, I intentionally limit his legal last name.

Frankly, a man who chose not to attend his own son's funeral does not get to benefit from legacy, association, or public sympathy. He forfeited that.

I said what I said. And I mean it.

The page took off quickly. Within a week, it had over a thousand followers and grew. People were paying attention. People in Kansas were curious. I kept seeing the same comments surface repeatedly.

"Oh yeah... whatever happened with that body found in the trunk?"

And the answer, publicly, was nothing.

So, I posted what I had.

I posted screenshots and timelines. I posted that Rylee had been shot. I asked for anyone with information to come forward. Not theatrically. Directly.

Around the same time, I contacted Missouri Crime Stoppers. Rylee's last known address—Trevor's house—was in Missouri. That's where these things start—the last known address. Setting that up was one of the most quietly destabilizing things I've ever done. Filling out forms asking for information about your murdered child, knowing the case wasn't solved, is not administrative; it is life-halting.

This put Rylee's face on a rotating billboard along I-70.

There was something unexpectedly comforting about that. People messaged me saying they had seen it. They noticed when it rotated from case to case. His name was out there, moving, not buried in a file.

Back to the phone call.

A mere few days after the Facebook page went live, my phone rang.

It was the District Attorney's Office.

Not after evidence. Not after waiting. Not after asking. Only after the silence became public.

And I was furious.

This was nearly eleven months after I had been told via email that the bulk of the investigation was complete and was being turned over for review.

That gap mattered.

Because suddenly, now that social media was involved, there was time for a phone call. After months of silence. After 2 years of restraint. I had been patient long before this. I didn't call every day. I didn't hover. I didn't make myself a problem. I gave space. I gave time. I trusted that restraint would be respected. It wasn't. It got me nothing.

The first concern was not my son—it was control.

I was told I needed to take down the information stating that Rylee had been shot. Because this was information that only the killer would know.

No, it wasn't.

It was printed in black and white on his death certificate. A public record. Gunshot wound to the head. Thermal burns.

That should have been my first undeniable clue of incompetence.

Not malice. Not strategy. Incompetence.

The fact that I had to explain their own documentation to them would have been almost forgettable if it weren't so infuriating. Instead of asking how this information hadn't already been communicated to me, they were concerned about optics.

That phone call did not feel like justice was catching up. It felt like obligation responding to pressure.

By then, I was no longer willing to confuse obligation with justice.

Their next request came casually. They wanted me to come into the office the following Thursday. For the first time, I felt it clearly—the shift. The containment.

This wasn't a coincidence. It was because of the Facebook page. After months of being given nothing, I was now being treated as though I had betrayed them. The hypocrisy would have been laughable if it hadn't been so telling.

They weren't finally talking because they chose to, but because I forced them.

No context. No acknowledgment of distance. No pause to ask where I lived. Just an assumption that I would bop across town and sit down like this was a routine meeting.

It was another quiet blow, one that said more than they probably realized.

They had no idea I didn't live there, which explained a lot.

When I told them I lived ten hours away, there was a brief recalibration. No embarrassment. No apology. Just logistics. The date shifted from December 21 to December 28.

So I waited through Christmas.

I don't remember that Christmas.

When I look at the pictures now, I can see myself in them—smiling, standing where I was supposed to stand. But I am not there. The smiles have no weight. No presence. I am elsewhere entirely.

After Christmas, I made the ten-hour drive to Leavenworth. I stayed in a hotel, got up early, and drove to the Justice Center.

That is the actual name of the building.

No irony intended, apparently.

Inside, I met the crime victim liaison. That title caught me off guard. Not because it was inaccurate, but because it was the first time anyone connected to the case seemed to recognize Rylee as a victim.

She knew him. Not just from this case. Rylee had not been immune to trouble. Leavenworth County had slapped his hand once or twice over the years. Knowing that she knew him outside of this moment mattered in a strange way. It humanized him in a system that otherwise felt determined to flatten him.

Then I met the attorney who would be prosecuting the case.

Chris Lyon.

There was a handshake. I'm sure there was a "sorry for your loss" as well. I don't remember it.

What I remember is the table; documents were spread out, and names were printed in black ink.

One name I recognized immediately: Marvelli.

A second name rang a bell: Jack. Cam had mentioned him more than once.

"I don't like or trust that fucker," Cam had said. "But Rylee said he's good." And Cam, despite the hesitation in his gut, accepted that.

That Jack's name had been circled four times on Cam's legal pad. Four. Not once. Not twice. Four deliberate circles. That mattered.

During the meeting, it was said more than once that a murder conviction would be *difficult*.

That statement slid easily into the real focus.

Drugs.

This case, I was told, was about drugs. More specifically, it was about RICO at the state level. They were pursuing what would potentially be the first state-level Racketeer Influenced and Corrupt Organizations Act conviction.

That was the priority.

The mention of drugs didn't surprise me. What was striking was how little time was spent explaining how the murder fit into any of it. I assumed they would give me more details—I was wrong.

I was shown a chart, a clean, impersonal chart outlining sentencing expectations based on prior charges combined with current drug charges. It read like a projection and not an account of a life taken.

It was here that I finally heard it from their side: the suspects were already in the county jail.

Not for murder.

That part mattered.

I already knew they were in jail. I knew the same way I had learned nearly everything else in this case, through the streets, through word of mouth, through names that kept resurfacing in conversations that were never meant for me but somehow found their way there anyway. I knew at least one of the names was tied to someone I believed was involved in my son's death. I did not know they were all connected.

I walked out of that meeting without a clear understanding of what a RICO case actually was. The only Rico I knew was a cop back in the day.

But I understood something else very clearly.

This was never centered on my son. It never had been.

Rylee wasn't the focus. He was the key to a different, more prestigious conviction. One that carried weight. One that made headlines.

I've asked myself whether his case would have gone this far without the drugs. Whether there would have been movement, urgency, resources. I don't have to wonder anymore.

I know the answer; it would be cold.

The Facebook page still exists. Not in the capacity it had when it started, but over time, it became something closer to a memorial. A place where his name could remain present and his life would not be reduced to a case number or a procedural outcome.

Justice, as it was defined by the system, was never achieved in my eyes, so there was no reason to close it.

I also use the page to share other cold cases. Some are unfamiliar. Some belong to families I've known or met over the years.

Cases that might otherwise stay buried in silence. My heart holds those families differently now. Not with pity, but with recognition. There is a particular understanding that only comes from living this, from carrying absence forward. Walking even part of that road changes you.

It changed me.

Rylee's case does not fit the usual definition of a cold case. Names exist. Involvement is not a mystery. What remains missing is precision. Accountability. Truth. We know who was part of it, but not exactly how and why. The version that has been allowed to stand bears little resemblance to what the evidence actually points toward.

That kind of unresolved knowing is its own form of silence. One that doesn't come from lack of information, but from the refusal to fully confront it.

After that first meeting in Leavenworth, there were a few more. Not many. Just enough to create the appearance of involvement.

Over the next four to six weeks, I was asked back a handful of times. Each time, I went. I rearranged my life, made the drive, and sat across from them in conference rooms that all looked the same. These meetings came only after the #Justiceforryleejames page went live, and the timing wasn't subtle. I hadn't become more relevant—just visible.

They used the word "progress" as if it carried weight.

But the meetings were brief. Contained. Carefully managed. Updates were offered, words filled the room, yet nothing ever felt anchored to my son. It felt procedural and obligatory. As though my presence was being tolerated rather than engaged.

What made it worse was what I already knew.

It had been nearly a year since I had received an impersonal email signed by a narcotics detective—not homicide—stating that the bulk of the investigation was complete. I was told the case had essentially been built. So now that I was being invited back to hear "updates," the disconnect was impossible to ignore. Whatever was being framed as forward motion felt rehearsed, not new. Spoken, but silent.

I don't remember which meeting it was when the shift happened, as they all blur together now. You would think I'd remember every detail, every room, every exchange. I don't. Trauma doesn't archive moments cleanly—it compresses them.

What I do remember is when I stopped listening and asked a question.

I hadn't come in with a list. Most of the time, I just listened. I nodded. I bit my lip. I let thin explanations pass without challenge. But in one of those meetings, somewhere in that stretch, I asked a very specific question.

Just one question.

And the room changed.

Eyes lifted from notepads. There was a pause. A recalibration. This kind of thing happens when someone realizes they've misjudged who's sitting across the table. In that moment, it was clear they hadn't expected that question from me.

My silence had been consistent. In that meeting, I broke it with a single inquiry.

Geofencing.

There wasn't a clear answer—there rarely was. But there was a pause.

Geofencing is not obscure. It is a standard investigative tool. It allows investigators to identify which cellular devices were present within a defined geographic area during a specific window of time. Not who owned them. Not what was said. Just which phones were there.

It is often used in arson cases and shootings. In violent crimes where the exact participants are unclear, but the location and timing are not.

In my son's case, the location and timing were known.

There was a car. There was fire. There was a video.

The Ring camera triggered in the dark, picking up movement the eye wouldn't have caught. Figures moving around a vehicle. The details weren't clear since it was night. And then, unmistakably, flames. Fire erupting where there had been only darkness moments before.

The footage does not show faces, which it doesn't need to. The fire tells the story. The timestamp anchors it. The presence of people is undeniable.

Geofencing could have shown which phones were present when the fire started. It could have established who was there when my son's body was set on fire.

When I asked about it, the tone changed. Not defensively. Not openly. But enough that I knew the question had landed differently. Enough that it was clear they hadn't expected it from me.

For two years, no one in charge of my son's case had taken the time to understand who they were dealing with. Not my background. Not my experience. Not my understanding of investigative procedure. They didn't have to, but you would think someone might have been curious.

Instead, they mistook restraint for ignorance; silence for absence.

That moment made something clear to me. While enormous effort had been spent building charges that looked good on paper, there had been an opportunity to answer a much simpler, more essential question.

Who was there?

The technology existed. The evidence existed. The fire existed.

And yet, no definitive answer was ever given.

That was the moment I stopped believing this was about oversight. Instead, I started to understand it as a choice.

Not because I am his mother, but because of the investigation, or more accurately, the absence of one. I will say this until the day I die: Leavenworth County was not interested in solving my son's murder. That conclusion is supported not by emotion, but by inaction. By what was delayed, ignored, minimized, or never pursued at all.

Somewhere along the way, it became clear they believed years behind bars for unrelated charges equaled justice. I am here to tell you it does not.

It meant nothing to them that no one was held responsible for the fact that I will never hear my son say "Mah!" again. Rylee was simply gone. His death was reduced to "drug-related," as if that label explained it, excused it, or closed the door on accountability. The lack of compassion was unmistakable. It wasn't hidden. It was structural. And it was disgusting.

What RICO Is, and Why It Mattered Here

RICO stands for the *Racketeer Influenced and Corrupt Organizations Act.* At its core, it allows prosecutors to charge people not just for a single crime, but for participating in an ongoing criminal enterprise (U.S. Department of Justice). Instead of proving who pulled the trigger, RICO focuses on patterns: who was connected to whom, how money moved, how drugs moved, who benefited, and who helped keep the operation running.

A state-level racketeering case is rare. Most people associate RICO with federal prosecutions. Securing a conviction at the state level carries significance. It demonstrates the ability to dismantle an entire network rather than isolate a single act. It also allows multiple charges to be bundled together under one umbrella, creating longer sentences without having to prove every element of every crime individually.

That matters because RICO is often easier to prove than murder.

A murder conviction requires precision. You must establish who did it, how they did it, and why, beyond a reasonable doubt. Evidence must align tightly. Witnesses must hold. Timelines must be exact.

RICO does not require that.

Under RICO, prosecutors can rely on communications, financial records, drug transactions, prior arrests, and association itself. The focus shifts from "what happened to one person" to "what was happening within the group." Responsibility becomes collective rather than specific.

And once a RICO conviction is secured, significant prison time follows.

From the outside, it can look like justice. People go to prison. Sentences are long. A case is marked "resolved."

But resolution is not the same as accountability.

A RICO conviction answers how a criminal network functioned. It does not answer who murdered my son. And once time is being served for something else, the urgency to answer that question fades.

In that framework, it can begin to feel like "good enough."

Not because a life mattered less, but because the system measured success differently than a mother does.

What never stopped landing wrong for me was this: five boys, all under twenty-two at the time of the murder, were charged under RICO statutes. Racketeering. Organized criminal enterprise. A legal framework designed for coordinated, hierarchical crime. Somehow, that was easier to prove than murder. Easier than naming responsibility for a life taken. Easier than holding anyone directly accountable for my son.

The logic was practical, I was told, and yes, I understand that RICO allowed for broader evidence. Patterns instead of moments. Associations instead of actions. With a conviction, time would be served. The State could claim resolution. But resolution is not the same as justice. And efficiency is not the same as truth.

What I understood about RICO came from the evidence presented in court and the conversations heard during the trial. Any interpretation here reflects what I witnessed and how I understood it at the time.

Chapter Ten

Showing Up and Staying Home

By this point, the routine was familiar: the drive, the courthouse, the security line, the same hallways, and the same rooms where time moved strangely, too fast in moments that mattered, almost unbearably slow in the ones that didn't.

Familiar faces began joining me on that walk into the courthouse. Jaime showed up whenever she could. Liz, I think, made every hearing, including the ones I couldn't. Their presence did not fix anything, but it anchored me. It reminded me that Rylee existed beyond paperwork. He mattered outside of legal language.

I could not attend every proceeding.

That truth hurt more than I expected. As Rylee's mom, I wanted to be at everything. Every hearing. Every motion. Every moment where his name might be spoken aloud. I wanted my presence to count for something, even if it changed nothing.

But I was also still a mother to my girls.

I had to find a balance between showing up for a son who was gone and staying present for the children who were still here. That calculation never felt fair. It felt like choosing which loss deserved attention on any given day. No one prepares you for this part, the one no one talks about.

That is where depression lives.

Not in the courtroom itself, but in the space between obligations. In the quiet decisions made alone. In the guilt that follows either choice. In knowing that no version of "enough" actually exists.

The proceedings continued. Motions were filed. Dates were set. Then moved. Again. The process kept going whether I was there or not. Somehow, that was both expected and devastating.

I learned to carry absence differently. To trust that even when I could not physically be present, my son was still there, in name, in record, in consequence. It wasn't comfort; it was survival.

And it was all leading somewhere.

Even if no one could yet say where.

The Inferno

Chapter Eleven

Inside the Courtroom

I thought long and hard about how to write this section.

I had rewritten it more times than any other section of this book. I was trying to find a way to present what happened in that courtroom without adding to the noise that already surrounds cases like this. I wanted it to be honest. I wanted it to be accurate. And I wanted it to make as much sense as possible out of what often felt like nonsense.

Each section unfolds the way I remember it.

What follows is drawn from one hundred seventy-two pages of notes I took during the trial, observations made in real time, details that stayed with me, and the way testimony landed when heard all at once.

This book has not been typical since the moment you opened it, and it will not be now.

This is what I saw. This is what I heard. This is what remained.

This chapter is structured deliberately. Not as a narrative meant to persuade and not as an argument meant to convince. It moves piece by piece, the same way the trial did. One section at a time. One version of events at a time.

If you have never been in a murder trial, it may not resemble what you expect. It is not constant drama or orderly progression. It is hours of listening, watching people you do not know, and absorbing information that arrives out of sequence and without context.

Attorneys move in and out. Conversations happen in whispers. Papers change hands. Testimony pauses and resumes. The weight of what is being discussed never leaves the room, but it exists alongside procedure, interruptions, and the slow mechanics of a system doing what it does.

This chapter does not attempt to correct that.

It documents it.

What follows is not a reconstruction. It is not hindsight. It is not speculation.

It is the trial as it unfolded, and how it landed when heard in full.

The Trials of the accused,

through a mothers eyes.

The Countdown

After more than two years of waiting, the trial finally had a date. A fixed point on the calendar. Non-negotiable. Immovable. A day that would arrive whether you were ready or not.

For so long, everything had existed in suspension. No answers. No movement. Just time passing in a way that felt both endless and stalled. The moment the date was set, that suspension ended.

The waiting changed shape.

There is a particular psychological weight that comes with a fixed date after prolonged uncertainty. Before, the waiting had been abstract. Painful, but uncontained. Once the trial was scheduled, it narrowed. Focused. Every day began to count down toward something specific, even though what that something would actually bring remained unclear.

Preparing to return to Leavenworth meant preparing to enter the place where everything had stalled. The town itself had never left my body. It lived in muscle memory, in the way my chest tightened at certain thoughts, in the way silence still carried a threat. Now I was being asked to go back not as a mother searching, but as a mother watching.

Anticipation built without clarity.

I did not know what the trial would answer. I did not know what it would resolve. I only knew it was supposed to mean something. This was the step we had been waiting for. The thing that followed the silence. The structure was designed to bring order to what had been shattered.

I hoped for justice without fully understanding the cost of that hope.

At the time, hope felt necessary. Almost automatic. A reflex. After so long without movement, the idea that something official was finally happening carried its own gravity. I had believed that participation alone would offer some form of relief. I thought that witnessing the process would feel stabilizing, and that being present would somehow restore balance.

What I did not yet understand was that hope is not neutral.

Hope requires endurance. It demands attention. It pulls you forward even when your body has already learned how to survive by staying still. It asks you to reopen doors that I closed for protection, not avoidance.

As the date approached, I began preparing in ways that were practical and entirely insufficient. Logistics. Travel. Childcare. What to wear. Where to sit. None of it addressed the actual task at hand, which was surviving the act of watching my son become evidence.

The countdown continued.

Each day moved closer to a room where I would be asked to listen, observe, and remain composed while strangers spoke about my child in pieces. A room where nothing I felt would change what was being said, but everything I felt would be carried home with me at the end of each day.

The trial had a start date; understanding what it would take from me did not.

From the beginning, I knew there were four potential suspects.

The investigation had been conducted; charges had been filed. The legal process had moved forward. And as it unfolded, one trial became the primary focus.

Not by my choice, but by the direction of the investigation itself.

Jack's trial became the center of this chapter, and ultimately, the center of this book, because that is where the State placed its weight. That is where the evidence was argued. That is where the narrative was built.

The focus here reflects the structure of the prosecution, not a narrowing of responsibility.

Preparing for the trial did not look like preparing for justice.

It looked like logistics.

I chose a hotel in the next town over. Not because it was better, but because it was farther. Distance mattered. Proximity to the courthouse felt dangerous in ways I couldn't yet articulate. I needed space between where we slept and where everything I was trying not to imagine would unfold.

The hotel had a pool. That part was intentional.

For Lily and Sadie, the days ahead were already going to be saturated with things they could not control. I needed something ordinary for them. Something familiar. Something that resembled childhood, even if only briefly and artificially. A pool meant noise that wasn't courtroom silence. It meant movement instead of sitting still with dread. It meant moments when they could be children without knowing exactly what was coming.

This was the balance I kept trying to strike.

Living in the present while bracing for impact.

Creating normalcy while fully aware that it was temporary.

Grief planning is strange in that way. You pack snacks and swimsuits for your children while preparing to hear details about how your other child was murdered. You check hotel reservations and confirm court times in the same breath. You decide what everyone will eat for dinner while knowing that sleep will be shallow, and mornings will arrive too quickly.

None of it feels real when you are doing it.

All of it feels necessary.

I did not tell the girls much. Not because I was avoiding the truth, but because there was no version of the truth that could have helped them. I focused on routines. Wake up times. Breakfast plans. Which swimsuit went with which towel. Small decisions that anchored us to something concrete.

Logistics became a kind of shield.

If I could manage the details, maybe I could manage the days.

This was not denial; it was containment.

I was trying to reduce the surface area of what could hurt them. Trying to hold the trauma at bay long enough for us to get through each day intact. Trying to survive what had not yet happened but was already closing in.

Preparing for the trial was not about readiness—it was about endurance.

And at that point, endurance looked like a hotel with a pool, a little distance from the courthouse, and the quiet hope that normal moments might still exist alongside what we were about to face.

The Jury

The courtroom itself did not announce what it was about to hold.

The walls were neutral. Tan. Intentionally unremarkable. The kind of room designed to be flexible enough for anything. The same space that, the day before, could have held an adoption hearing or a wedding ceremony. The same bench. The same seal on the wall. The same chairs arranged with quiet precision.

Nothing in the room signaled that a murder trial was about to begin.

That neutrality was not accidental—it was institutional. It was a reminder that the system does not change its posture based on the weight of what it carries. The room stays the same, even though the people inside it do not.

Jury selection began without ceremony.

Roughly thirty people were called in—
ordinary citizens. They filed into the box and
the surrounding seats with the uncertainty of
people who knew they were stepping into
something serious but had no way of knowing
how serious it would become.

They looked like anyone you might pass at
a grocery store or sit next to at a school event.
Different ages. Different backgrounds.
Different levels of comfort in the space. Some
sat upright and alert. Others slouched slightly,
arms crossed, trying not to draw attention.

None of them knew what they were about
to see.

One by one, they were questioned. Not
about guilt or innocence yet, but about
availability, about hardship. About whether
they could set aside personal beliefs and
follow instructions. About whether they could

handle graphic material without becoming overwhelmed.

Some answered confidently. Some hesitated. Some avoided eye contact entirely.

You could watch the moment when it dawned on a few of them that this was not a case they would simply listen to and then forget, that whatever they were selected for would follow them home at night.

Slowly, the group narrowed.

Thirty became twenty.

Twenty became fifteen.

Fifteen became thirteen.

Twelve jurors, one alternate.

The people who remained did not look relieved; they looked sober. It was as if something had quietly settled onto their shoulders.

I remember noticing details I never would have paid attention to before.

One juror kept twisting a wedding ring around their finger whenever the word "fire" was mentioned. Another sat perfectly still, hands folded, eyes fixed forward, as if movement itself might invite responsibility they were not ready to accept.

There was a younger man who nodded along too quickly, eager, perhaps, to show he understood. A middle-aged woman who took notes during *voir dire*, as if already preparing herself for what was coming. An older juror who stared at the floor more than the attorneys, only looking up when directly addressed.

One juror excused themselves entirely.

They stood, voice shaking, and said they could not do it. That they were not equipped to sit through what was being described. That it would be too much.

They were thanked, then released.

The rest stayed.

At some point, I realized something that would stay with me long after the trial had ended.

These people did not come here knowing they would be shown images of my son's body. They did not arrive prepared to hear how he died. They did not volunteer to carry this.

They had been summoned for civic duty. And now, without fully understanding how it happened, they were about to be entrusted with the aftermath of my son's death.

When the final group was seated, the room shifted.

Not dramatically—subtly.

The chatter stopped. The air changed. The attorneys adjusted their posture. The judge's tone sharpened, just slightly.

This was no longer preparation.

This was the beginning.

As I watched these strangers take their places, I wondered how many of them would leave this room changed in ways they could not yet imagine. How many would carry pieces of this trial into their own lives? How many would struggle later to explain what they had seen, without breaking some unspoken rule about how much truth is acceptable to share?

They did not know my son.

But they were about to be asked to hold him anyway.

Support in the Court Room

I do not remember the drive to the justice center. I do not remember parking or walking up to the building. Those pieces are gone. What remains feels muted, as if everything happened underwater. Sounds were dulled. Movements were slowed. Recognition seemed to arrive half a second late, like my mind was struggling to keep up with what my body was already enduring.

The courthouse itself was familiar. I had been walking into this building for years. The hallways, the doors, the metal detectors, the quiet authority of the space. None of it was new. And yet, that morning, it felt altered. Heavier. Charged with something irreversible.

By the time we arrived, security already knew who I was.

They knew the date; they knew why it mattered.

Walking inside did not feel like entering a building. It felt like crossing a line I had been circling for more than two years.

Faces began to register slowly: Liz, Jaime. The relief was immediate and physical, a release in my chest I hadn't realized was locked tight. The simple knowledge that I would not sit through this alone mattered more than anything else in that moment.

Sydney was beside me. Steady. Present. We had been counting down to this date together, marking time on calendars and in conversations, but standing there made the countdown real in a way that numbers never did.

Then there were others: Stacy, Jessica. Trevor and Cam.

Stacy was a wrestling mom long before she was someone who I would come to consider my sister. We spent weekends in the bleachers together, watching our sons wrestle, learning about each other in the in-between moments that happen when life is loud and ordinary at the same time. Those mats, those gyms, those long days built something real. Her presence in that courtroom carried all of that history with it.

Jessica was there from the very beginning of my life in Leavenworth. I was a fresh Army wife, and she was married to one of Tom's soldiers. Without hesitation, she welcomed me into a life I hadn't yet learned how to live. From the moment we were stationed there, she became my friend, not conditionally, not temporarily, and she remains my friend still. Seeing her in that room reminded me that some bonds survive moves, losses, and years of silence without effort.

They were not just support in that moment—they were continuity. Proof that my life existed before this courtroom and would somehow continue after it.

There were other faces too. People who had known me since we moved to Leavenworth. People who understood the gravity of that room without needing it explained. People who showed up not because it was expected, but because they intended to be there.

Some faces surprised me; others didn't. Every one of them mattered.

And then slowly, I saw them.

Women from Rylee's past. Former girlfriends. Familiar smiles, older now. Lives continued. Relationships built. Children mentioned quietly or held close. Partners standing beside them. Families already formed.

I was not prepared for that moment.

It hit all at once, sharp and unfiltered. A realization I had somehow managed to avoid until then. My son would never have that. The life he talked about. The family he wanted. The future that was already taking shape for people who once loved him.

They had moved forward, as life demands. They had children. Stability. Ordinary chaos. A future that unfolds naturally when time is allowed to continue.

Rylee would never stand where they stood.

He would never become a father.

Never build a family of his own.

Never to become the man he was determined to be.

It was grief layered on top of grief. Not louder, but deeper. Quieter. It settles into the body without asking for permission.

I watched these women exist in lives that continued, and for the first time, I felt the full weight of what was stolen from him—not just what was taken from me. It wasn't only that he was gone. It was that his future had been erased so completely that other people were now living it in his absence.

That realization stayed with me as we took our seats.

The room filled slowly. Conversations remained hushed. Hugs were brief, careful, as if everyone understood there were no right words yet. Or maybe there never would be.

And then the testimony began.

As details surfaced, I started watching the people around me fall apart. Not dramatically. Not loudly. But visibly. Shoulders folding inward. Hands covering mouths. Eyes filling and spilling over.

They were absorbing what happened to Rylee in real time, hearing it laid out clinically. Sequentially. Without softness.

And I wasn't crying.

That realization landed almost as hard as the others.

Grief is strange like that. I was watching people mourn my son in ways I hadn't yet allowed myself to. Tears came to them easily, instinctively. What I felt instead was distance. Stillness. A containment that felt unnatural even as it held me together.

The medic part of me understood. Dissociation has a purpose. It happens when the body knows it cannot process everything all at once. It is protection. Control. Function.

But another part of me wondered what was wrong with me.

Why couldn't I cry?

Why wasn't my body responding the way theirs were?

I sat there watching people break open while I remained intact, almost too intact. Present, but removed. Aware, but buffered.

It felt like knowing grief would be delayed.

It was as if my body had decided this was not yet the moment.

I did not know then that grief would find its way in later, in other forms, at other times. I only knew that sitting in that room, surrounded by people who cared enough to hurt, I felt both grateful and deeply unsettled.

The trial had begun.

And already, it was nothing like I expected.

Rhythm of Trial

There is no assigned seating in this courtroom.

By the time Jack's trial began, I already knew who his parents were. They sat directly in front of me. Close enough that I could read the tag on their collars. Close enough that I could hear them breathe.

I felt no anger toward them. No animosity. So there was no need to look away.

I felt for them in the same way I felt for myself.

None of us wanted to be here. None of us had asked for this version of our lives. We were all seated in the same room for different reasons, bound together by something none of us could undo.

The rhythm of the trial began the same way every day.

We were asked to stand. Then to sit. The judge entered. The room shifted into its formal posture. And then the defendant was brought in.

Less than ten feet from me.

He was shackled. Restrained. He looked like an ordinary young man. Not a monster. Not visibly dangerous. Not marked in any obvious way by what he was accused of having done.

This was the person the State said was responsible for murdering my son.

I had spent years inside courtrooms through my work, but only in fragments. As a witness, only in short appearances, but never like this. Never for hours at a time. Never sitting still while something irreversible unfolded, piece by piece.

This was not the rigid, hushed environment people imagine when they think of a courtroom.

It was procedural. Interruptible. Human in ways that felt wrong.

People whispered. Attorneys leaned in close to one another, murmuring behind folders. Papers were passed. Someone bent down to speak quietly into another attorney's ear. People entered and exited through side doors with little disruption.

I could hear gum being chewed too loudly somewhere behind me. Snacks being opened. A can of soda popped and poured. Tissues passed from hand to hand.

All of this happened while my son's death was being discussed.

The judge listened to everything and watched everything, corrected small things, and allowed others to pass without comment.

The structure held, but it was not reverent. It was functional.

Opening statements began with force.

A body was found in a burning car.

That was how it started. Direct. Graphic. Immediate.

For a brief moment, I felt something close to relief. A flicker of belief that this was about justice for Rylee. That the truth was going to be pursued fully and without hesitation. That what followed would match the weight of that opening.

But that intensity was a hook.

As testimony continued, it stopped and started. Momentum had been stalled. Threads were introduced and then abandoned. Details surfaced without context. Important moments passed without emphasis.

What began with fire slowly dissolved into fragments.

And all the while, we were there. We stood when told and sat when told. Listening. Watching.

Jack's parents remained in front of me. The defendant remained within reach. The judge remained observant. The jury remained attentive.

And the room continued on in its strange, ordinary cadence.

This was the rhythm of the trial.

Not dramatic. Not continuous. Not cohesive.

A series of starts and stops. Of gravity interrupted by routine. Of devastating information delivered alongside the mechanics of a system that does not pause for what it carries.

This was not a performance—it was an experience.

And once it began, there was no way to step outside of it.

When the Court Adjourned

By the end of the first day, I was told the trial could last one to two days.

At first, that seemed impossible. How could the murder of my son be presented in just a day or two? How could something that had taken over my life for years be compressed into such a short span of time?

But after sitting through the entire day, I understood it differently.

We listened for seven solid hours. An hour break for lunch, and then back into the same chairs, the same room, the same cadence. Detectives testified. Evidence was introduced. The State laid out its case, piece by piece, without pause. It was long. It was exhausting. It was heavy in a way that does not register until you are living in it.

I gained a new respect for trials that stretch on for weeks. I do not know how anyone could absorb this day after day without breaking in ways no one can see. How many times can the same facts be repeated? How often can the same words be spoken aloud before they lose their shape?

I am aware that I repeat myself in this book. I know it as I write it. But this is how it happened. This is how it lived in me. It circled back again and again, just as it has since the first phone call. Editing it out feels dishonest. When something returns this often, it is because it never left.

When the day ended, we shuffled out of the courtroom and down the stairs. We made plans for dinner. I made a few phone calls to people who were waiting for updates, trying to translate something that did not translate easily.

It was not lost on me that while my life was actively changing, recalibrating itself around what I was hearing, for everyone else it was simply the end of a workday. Another evening. Another plan. Another tomorrow that looked mostly like today.

That dissonance stayed with me.

Each day of the trial ended this way. Not with resolution. Not with relief. But with the quiet understanding that the world keeps moving, even as something in you shifts permanently.

The trial was not just something I attended.

It was something I carried with me when I left.

CHAPTER TWELVE

The Evidence

The Body

My son's body as evidence was not presented first. It came after lunch.

We left the courtroom for the break knowing what was coming, though no one had said it out loud. When we returned, Lorelai, my victim advocate, stopped me before I could sit. She did not speak as a representative of the court or the prosecution, but as a person who understood what was about to happen.

She told me to prepare myself.

I have criticized many parts of this process, but she had never failed me. Not once.

When the courtroom settled and the lights dimmed, the first image appeared on the screen from across the room. I was seated roughly ten feet away. At first, I could not tell what I was looking at. It was a burned vehicle on the side of a rural road. Its exterior was blackened and warped. The trunk was open. There was something inside it, but from that distance, it did not register as a body.

It did not register as my son.

The next image was closer.

What I saw was not immediately recognizable as human. It was the outline of a body, but without features. No arms. No lower legs. Those are often burned completely to ash in fires of this intensity. There was no blood to speak of. Just gray. White. Black.

What remained was shape.

I could see where his mouth had been, where his eyes were sunken. It was not quite a skull, but it was no longer a face. If you have ever seen a poorly done movie prop meant to represent a burned body, something that looks artificial because it is so damaged it stops resembling a person, that is the closest comparison I can make.

Except this was not a prop.

This was what was left of my son.

I did not react the way people expect a mother would. I did not scream. I did not cry. I did not leave the room. I stared, trying to understand what I was seeing. My brain could not immediately reconcile that image with the child I had raised.

Later, I would realize that this dissociation was the only reason I was able to sit there at all.

The medical examiner testified to extensive thermal damage. The body had been exposed to extreme heat for a prolonged period. Soft tissue was largely destroyed. Extremities were absent. What remained was described clinically, without pause, without acknowledgment of who this body had once been.

Cause of death was addressed.

A gunshot wound was identified. The wound was to the head. Due to the condition of the remains, the exact trajectory could not be fully reconstructed, but the presence of the injury was clear. In my own understanding, based on my experience and the nature of the injury, Rylee was more than likely dead or at least unconscious at the time of the fire.

That distinction matters.

Time of death could not be precisely determined. Fire complicates timelines. Heat alters tissue and erases markers typically used to estimate when death occurred. As a result, the interval between the gunshot and the fire could not be established definitively.

The examiner did not testify to defensive wounds.

The examiner did not testify to signs of restraint.

The examiner did not testify to indicators of a struggle.

Not because those things were ruled out, but because the condition of the body made such determinations unreliable.

That nuance was stated quietly.

The jury was shown images. Not many, but enough.

No one spoke about who Rylee was before he became evidence. There was no mention of his age beyond what was required. There was no pause to acknowledge that the remains on the screen belonged to a twenty-one-year-old man who had been alive less than two days earlier.

The body was introduced as proof.

And then the trial moved on.

The Gunshot Wound

The image appeared without ceremony.

My son's torso was laid out on a blue medical pad, the kind used in exam rooms and autopsies to create contrast and control. The background was sterile; the lighting was flat. Everything about the image was designed to remove emotion.

The skullcap had been cut away. The top of his head was open, sectioned cleanly, exposing what was meant to be examined rather than mourned. Measurements were overlaid on the image: numbers, angles, distances.

The entrance wound was identified. The exit wound was identified. Trajectory was discussed as if the body on the screen were anonymous, interchangeable, and instructional.

There were no identifying features left to anchor him as human. No expression. No context. Just tissue rendered into evidence, charted, and labeled.

The examiner spoke in precise terms. Location. Path. Cause. The language was exact, unemotional, and practiced. It was the language of someone doing her job properly, and it landed with the weight of finality.

I stared at the screen trying to understand what I was seeing. I knew, because I had been told, that this was my son. But the image itself did not resemble the boy I raised. It resembled a diagram—a specimen—something closer to a medical illustration than a person.

And yet, this was him.

I did not react. I did not move. I was aware of the room in a way that felt unfamiliar. Every sound seemed sharper, every pause longer. I could feel attention shift, not toward the screen, but toward me.

If anyone in that courtroom had not known who I was before, they knew now.

I understood what was being explained. The measurements made sense. The description was clear. The process was familiar.

What did not make sense was the stillness of my own body.

There was no collapse. No outward response. Just the quiet realization that my son's body had been reduced to a clinical image, and that I was watching it happen.

The fire was introduced as evidence after the body.

That sequence mattered, even if no one said it out loud.

By the time testimony turned to the fire, the jury had already been shown what remained of my son. What followed, according to the State, was meant to explain how thoroughly everything else had been destroyed.

Testimony came from W.L., a firefighter with the Kickapoo Fire Department. A volunteer department. A small crew. The kind that responds when something burns far from town because no one else is close enough to arrive first.

Firefighters were responding to a vehicle fire, not a death.

The call came in during the early morning hours. It was a report of a car burning on a county road. Remote. No nearby structures. No witnesses were waiting to explain what they were seeing. By the time the department arrived, the fire was already well established.

W.L. described the vehicle as fully involved, flames consuming the interior, flames extending into the trunk area. The heat was intense enough that standard suppression took time to gain control. This was not a surface fire. Not a brief ignition or a contained engine fire. It was a sustained burn.

Firefighters worked the scene until the flames were extinguished, and the area was safe enough to approach. What remained of the vehicle showed extensive heat damage throughout. The trunk area had been compromised. Metal warped and deformed.

Materials were reduced to ash. Plastic, fabric, wiring, and upholstery were consumed.

The size and intensity of the fire stood out even to the experienced responders. It was described as one of the larger vehicle fires encountered, particularly given the isolated location and lack of surrounding ignition sources.

Once suppression was complete, the vehicle was secured. The contents were no longer recognizable as individual items. Anything combustible had been consumed. Anything that might have held trace evidence had been altered beyond recovery by extreme heat.

During post-fire assessment, damage to the rear of the vehicle was immediately apparent. The taillights had melted away. The trunk structure had failed. Through that damage, responders observed what appeared to be human remains inside the trunk.

At that point, the scene changed.

Law enforcement was notified. What had begun as a response to a vehicle fire transitioned into a death investigation.

Investigators later testified to the condition of the vehicle. Severe thermal destruction. Limited recoverable material. No intact interior. No usable surfaces untouched by heat.

This mattered.

Because fire does not just destroy what is visible.

It destroys timelines. It destroys context. It destroys answers before questions are ever asked.

The fire explained why there were gaps. Why so much was missing. Why certain things could not be determined with certainty.

Why reconstruction was limited. Why conclusions relied on what came from outside the scene rather than from it.

It was also the reason the case leaned so heavily on everything else: phone records, digital trails, drug activity, and witness testimony.

Because the fire had erased most of what could have spoken for itself.

There was no evidence presented tying the fire to a specific accelerant purchase. No receipts. No gas station footage. There was no timeline showing when fuel may have been obtained or by whom. No explanation was offered for how the fire was started beyond the assertion that it was intentional.

The fire was treated as a fact, not a question.

A result, not a process.

Once the vehicle was removed, what remained at the scene was minimal. Ash. Scorch marks. A stretch of county road that returned to silence once the equipment left.

The jury was shown photographs of the burned vehicle. Blackened metal. Collapsed structure. A shape that no longer resembled something meant to transport a person.

The fire was large enough to register on a Ring camera miles away. Not faces. Not details. Just movement and light against darkness.

And yet, despite its scale, the fire stood oddly alone in the case.

It explained destruction, but not decisions. It explained loss, but not sequence.
It explained why answers were missing, but not why no one pressed harder for the ones that may still have been possible.

The fire burned long enough to consume evidence.

It burned long enough to erase clarity.

And then it went out.

What it left behind was not proof.

It was absence.

The House

The residence was a tan duplex. Nothing about it stood out. It was the kind of place deputies visited every day. Ordinary. Unremarkable. A structure that blended into the background of routine calls and paperwork.

A sheriff's deputy testified that he first went there to serve eviction paperwork. At that time, there was nothing notable to report. The house appeared occupied. It did not present as a crime scene. There were no visible signs of violence, no damage noted, and nothing that suggested anything more than a normal residence being lived in.

It was routine. Just another address.

He later returned as part of his normal follow-up. By then, the house appeared abandoned. The change was significant enough that he commented on it in his testimony. The space no longer felt lived in. He described it as a flophouse—vacated abruptly, disturbed, used, but not maintained.

During this second visit, blood was observed.

A photograph was introduced at trial showing blood on a wall located in the kitchen, dripping downward from the ceiling above. The image came from body-camera footage. It was shown briefly. There was no extended explanation. No context was offered beyond its existence.

And then it moved on.

There was no testimony about any follow-up at the property. No indication that investigators had contacted the property owner. No evidence was presented that anyone had asked whether repairs were required, whether damage was discovered, or whether anything inside the home had been altered or removed.

There was no testimony about collecting samples. No mention of luminol testing. No explanation of whether the area above the drip had been examined. No documentation was offered showing attempts to trace where the blood originated.

The image exists.

Later testimony established that after Rylee was killed, the house remained active. People continued to come and go. The space was used.

The blood was not reported until after the final eviction visit. What happened in that window of time was never explained.

The questions raised were *never* addressed.

Photographs were shown of walls. A mattress was photographed standing upright, a couch standing on its end, and a sink of dirty dishes. There were no images presented of the area above where the blood was seen dripping. No documentation of a floor being examined, no nearby wall or floor identified as the source, no evidence of blood spatter, and no indication that any portion of the structure was removed or tested.

There was also no documentation indicating whether that area had been altered prior to law enforcement's arrival, let alone examined afterward.

Blood was presented, but not as evidence. Nothing was established about where it came from.

What is striking is not what was shown, but what seemed not to be asked.

This next observation is mine alone.

Blood does not drip through a ceiling into another room without originating from *somewhere* specific. For it to travel downward, there must be a source. That source should have been identifiable, documentable, and testable.

Whether that was done was never explained.

The house appears briefly in the record, raises questions, and then disappears from it.

The house where my son was killed was never treated as a focal point. It remained a place referenced, but not examined; present in testimony, but absent in detail.

It was one more clear indication that this case was not built around his murder.

The investigation did not narrow down to the murder; it expanded outward into something else.

What followed was not a reconstruction of how my son died, but a sustained, methodical investigation into how drugs moved, who moved them, and how often.

This part of the case was not rushed.

Law enforcement had spent months observing patterns. Phones were monitored. Movements were tracked. Communications were watched over time, not in isolation. Investigators testified to long hours spent reviewing data, mapping connections, and following behavior across days, weeks, and jurisdictions.

This was not a casual observation, but a sustained surveillance.

Tracking data was introduced, showing how individuals moved from place to place. Locations were logged. Timelines were built. Investigators described watching repeated travel routes and repeated contacts, identifying consistency that pointed to coordination rather than coincidence.

Phones were not just seized but were examined in depth.

Investigators explained how data extraction works. How deleted messages can still be recovered. How timestamps are verified. How platforms are cross-referenced to confirm identity and intent. Testimony walked the jury through how they verified who was communicating with whom, when, and for what purpose.

This work took time.

It took personnel.

It took resources.

Rylee was present in this evidence.

His phone appeared in the timelines. His name appeared in message threads. He was part of the communications that were tracked, reviewed, and presented. He was not omitted from this investigation, and I will not omit him here.

Messages between Jack, Marvellis, Tyler, Jayden, and Rylee were shown with dates and times clearly marked. Conversations spanned weeks and months. They discussed quantities, pricing, logistics, and delivery. They referenced sourcing drugs from out of state and transporting them across state lines.

Investigators testified to how these messages were corroborated with movement data. When messages referenced travel, location data matched. When delivery was discussed, patterns aligned. When money was mentioned, accounts and transactions were examined.

This was not speculation.

This was a correlation built over time.

Law enforcement also described monitoring activity after my son's death. Phones did not go quiet. Messages continued. Plans continued. Drug activity continued. This included testimony about the use of online platforms and the dark web to obtain substances, including Xanax shipped to Jack's parents' house.

That evidence was presented carefully. Step by step. Screenshot by screenshot.

Investigators explained how long it took to piece this together. How much review was required. How many hours were spent observing, documenting, and confirming before anything was ever presented in court.

This was a thorough investigation.

It was disciplined.

It was organized.

It was technically sound.

And it was focused.

What it did not focus on was equally clear.

There were no comparable hours described for tracking the movement of my son's body.

No comparable timelines reconstructing the interior of the house.

No comparable forensic follow through on blood evidence.

The energy went where evidence could be aggregated, quantified, and charged.

The digital evidence told a complete and compelling story. It demonstrated coordination. Conspiracy. Distribution. Profit.

It proved a drug case.

And in that work, the investigators did their job.

What it did not do was answer how my son was killed, who pulled the trigger, or why the physical evidence surrounding his death was never pursued with the same rigor.

That distinction matters.

Because this was not a lack of capability— it was a matter of direction.

This was the case they built.

This was the case they tried.

This was the case they ultimately won.

Everything else existed around it.

It was during this testimony that something else finally made sense. I understood the initial meeting differently than I ever had before. The one that came only after my Facebook page forced their invitation. The one where they laid out potential sentencing ranges tied to past convictions and associated conduct.

At the time, I listened, but I did not hear it. It sounded like noise. It was like Charlie Brown's teacher talking past me while I waited for answers about my son.

Sitting in that courtroom, the bubble finally popped. I heard what they had been telling me from the beginning.

There was no intent to win a murder charge; they did not believe they could. What they believed they could win was a drug case. And so that is what they built.

They did not pivot away from the murder, but they never fully moved toward it. Somewhere along the way, solving my son's death stopped being an objective at all. It became a charge added to the structure of a case that was already moving in a different direction.

I thought a charge of murder meant something. I thought it meant the same effort would be made, even if the outcome was uncertain. That the results would be left to a jury. I did not understand that the decision had already been made to pursue what could be won, rather than what needed to be answered.

In their framework, the prosecution believed decades of sentencing equaled justice.

It does not.

The thoroughness of the digital evidence stood in contrast to the lack of clarity surrounding the circumstances of Rylee's death.

Justice for a murder requires responsibility. It requires a genuine effort to establish who took a life and to present that case with the same rigor as any other charge. Although a murder charge existed on paper, it was never pursued with that level of intent.

The case that was built made a conviction on that charge impossible.

The decision to focus on what could be secured rather than what needed to be answered was made long before I understood it was being made.

I am not saying I was lied to. I was told the case would involve RICO. What I did not understand—and what was never fully explained to me—was what that meant for my son.

I didn't know what to ask. I didn't know what to expect. I trusted the process.

I was not looking for a broader case. I was looking for accountability.

That is where the disconnect was.

There were only two witnesses. What follows is taken directly from their testimonies—no more, no less. If it feels incomplete, that is because it was.

The first was Marvellis.

He was the only witness who had claimed firsthand knowledge of how Rylee was killed. Every assertion about the shooting—its location, the alleged motive, and what happened afterward—originated with him. No other witness had testified to seeing the shooting. No forensic expert independently reconstructed the scene he had described. The murder charge rested entirely on his account.

Marvellis testified that Jack shot Rylee. He told the jury that the shooting occurred inside the residence, and he was present when it happened. He described the wound as being to

Rylee's neck. According to his testimony, Rylee was shot inside the house while he was sleeping upstairs in a bedroom.

He attributed the shooting to a drug-related dispute. At various points, the explanation for why the shooting occurred shifted. It was described as a disagreement over money Rylee was owed for cannabis, a broader financial dispute, betrayal tied to money being used elsewhere, or retaliation.

The motive was not anchored to a single, consistent cause but moved within the broader context of drug activity and personal conflict.

Marvellis further testified that after the shooting, efforts were made to clean the scene. He described bleach being used. He claimed that the carpet was cut. He asserted that the interior of the house had been altered to remove evidence of what had happened. He also testified that other individuals were involved in moving Rylee's body in the events that followed.

These details created a vivid narrative of a crime scene and its aftermath. The testimony described a shooting inside a residence followed by deliberate efforts to erase it. It suggested planning, intent, and concealment. A scenario that would ordinarily generate extensive physical evidence under even the most routine investigative standards.

What it did not provide was proof.

As with the earlier testimony from the sheriff who observed the blood, these gaps remained unaddressed. Following Marvellis's testimony, no additional clarification was provided—neither by the State nor through witness testimony.

No forensic evidence was presented to corroborate the claim that a shooting occurred inside the home. There was no blood pattern analysis introduced to establish where Rylee was shot or whether a shooting occurred there at all. No reconstruction of the interior was offered to the jury. There were no measurements, diagrams, or expert testimony explaining how the physical space supported the narrative being told.

There was no evidence tying Rylee's body to that location. No transfer evidence. No forensic linkage connecting his remains to the interior of the house. No timeline reconstructing how long his body was allegedly inside the residence or how investigators verified the sequence of events described by the witness.

The alleged cleanup efforts were not substantiated. There was no documentation showing when or how those actions were discovered. There was no testimony that the rental company had been contacted regarding repairs or damage consistent with a violent crime. No invoices. No repair records. No confirmation that damage requiring remediation had been reported or addressed.

The jury was not shown photographs of the floor or interior space where Rylee was said to have been shot. There were no images of the residence had been introduced to anchor the testimony to a physical reality. The location of the alleged killing remained unseen.

What made that absence more striking was the contrast with the evidence that did exist. The same individuals described as capable of executing a near-perfect crime scene cleanup were also the subjects of an investigation built almost entirely from digital evidence. Phones documented communication, coordination, and transactions. Messages were preserved. Records were retained. Drugs were ordered and delivered directly to residences. The trail was extensive and easily discoverable.

The idea that this same group left behind a detailed, traceable record of criminal activity across multiple devices, yet somehow eliminated all physical evidence of a violent shooting inside a home, required a level of sophistication that did not reflect anywhere else in the case.

Marvellis's testimony also conflicted with the medical evidence already presented to the jury. His description of the wound did not align with the medical examiner's testimony that had been introduced earlier. That discrepancy was not reconciled through expert explanation or forensic clarification. Jurors were left holding incompatible accounts without guidance on how they could coexist.

In addition to his claims about the murder, Marvellis was positioned within the broader drug case. His testimony included references to pills being sorted and re-bagged, to blue pills being present, and to drugs moving between individuals. Jurors heard about pills leaving with one person and not returning. These details reinforced the State's drug narrative, but they did not independently support the murder charge.

The court also heard testimony that complicated the State's portrayal of motive. Less than twenty-four hours before Rylee's death, evidence showed that Rylee helped Marvellis's brother during a medical emergency by calling for an ambulance when it was needed. That fact stood in contrast to a narrative rooted solely in betrayal, retaliation, or rage. It reflected proximity, familiarity, and a relationship that did not align neatly with the idea of an imminent, intentional killing driven by hostility or debt.

That contrast deepened when paired with the circumstances of Rylee's death. According to the testimony, he was sleeping at the time he was shot. This detail did not fit the image of someone who believed he was in immediate danger. It stood in tension with his final text messages, which showed that he knew things were getting bad. People, especially Rylee, do not sleep in the home of someone they believe is betraying them.

Throughout Marvellis's testimony, responsibility appeared fluid. The narrative shifted depending on the question being asked and the context in which it was answered. His account was not stabilized by corroborating witnesses or anchored by physical evidence. The jury was asked to evaluate the most serious charge in the case based almost entirely on credibility alone.

The State asked Marvellis to carry the act of killing, the motive, the location, and the aftermath. It asked for his testimony to stand in for forensic reconstruction, physical proof, and independent confirmation.

This was their only foundation for the murder charge.

As soon as Marvellis was escorted out of the courtroom by the bailiffs, the State called its next witness.

There was no pause. No reframing. No attempt to reinforce the narrative that had just been presented. The transition was immediate.

This witness did not testify to seeing the shooting. There was no claim of being present inside the house or a firsthand account of how Rylee was killed. Instead, the testimony focused on a statement allegedly made by Marvellis within hours of Rylee's death.

According to the witness, Marvellis admitted responsibility for the killing. The testimony was direct. Marvellis allegedly said to this witness that he "shot that boy."

This statement was not made days later, after arrest or negotiation; it was attributed to him in the immediate aftermath of the murder, before narratives had hardened and before courtroom strategies existed.

The impact of this testimony was immediate.

The State had just relied on Marvellis as the sole witness accusing Jack of pulling the trigger. His credibility was the foundation of the murder charge. By introducing testimony that Marvellis had previously claimed responsibility for the killing himself, the State placed two irreconcilable accounts before the jury.

There was no way to reconcile them. Either Marvellis was telling the truth in court, or he was telling the truth when the statement was made hours after the murder. Both could not be true.

Reasonable doubt did not need to be argued. It was introduced by the State, through its own witness, *immediately* after presenting the only testimony that supported a murder conviction directed at Jack.

In that moment, the outcome became unavoidable. Whatever uncertainty had existed before was now fixed. The murder charge no longer rested on competing interpretations. It rested on a contradiction the State itself had placed into evidence.

No later testimony could repair that fracture.

The question of who was responsible for Rylee's death was no longer unclear; it was unprovable.

I did not need to embellish anything to understand what had just happened.

I sat there realizing that the State had just dismantled its own murder case. Not through defense argument, not through cross-examination, but through its own choices.

Through the sequence of witnesses that it presented.

What I felt in that moment was not confusion—it was betrayal.

For more than two years, they told me they were working on my son's case. I believed that meant his murder was being pursued with intention, even if the outcome was uncertain. I believed the facts would be tested, weighed, and left to a jury. Instead, I watched the State introduce testimony that made a murder conviction impossible, and do so without hesitation.

I remember thinking, are they hearing what they're saying?

It was not subtle, nor was it complex. The contradiction was immediate and absolute. And yet, it was presented anyway, as if no one in the room who mattered would question it.

In that moment, I understood something I had not allowed myself to understand before. It was not about guilt, but about direction. The murder charge existed, but it was never protected. It was never carried, never given the same care as the case the State actually intended to win.

I felt exposed. I felt used. I felt like a spectator to a process that had been happening around me, not with me, all along.

Justice, I realized, was not being defined by truth. It was being defined by outcome.

That was the moment I understood that no one was going to be held responsible for my son's death.

Tyler's trial came later, after the verdicts had been returned and the sentences imposed. I did not expect to learn anything new by sitting through it. I believed whatever decisions had been made were already final.

I was wrong.

During Tyler's trial, Marvellis testified again. This time, it was not the State asking the questions.

Tyler's defense attorney did not treat Marvellis as a neutral witness. The tone was accusatory. The questioning carried an assumption that had never been voiced during Jack's case.

Not as a claim. Not as a charge. But as something already understood.

The implication was unmistakable. Marvellis was being questioned not as someone who merely witnessed what happened, but as someone whose role in Rylee's death was being directly challenged.

The attorney pressed him directly, not gently, not hypothetically. The question was framed as a confrontation, not an inquiry. Marvellis was asked whether he had received a deal in exchange for his testimony.

That was how I learned, definitively, that Marvellis would never go to trial for Rylee's murder. Even having lived adjacent to systems like this, I believed I would be informed when decisions of that magnitude were made.

I wasn't.

The agreement with Marvellis happened without my knowledge. There was no conversation, no explanation—just a shift I had to learn about after the fact.

I didn't expect to have a say in what they decided. But I also didn't expect to be blindsided by it.

No explanation had been offered to me before that moment. No acknowledgment. No transparency. The fact surfaced only because another defendant's attorney forced it into the open, in a courtroom, on the record.

That silence did not end there. I was not contacted afterward. No one explained the terms of the deal, the scope of it, or how it factored into the case that had already been tried. No one clarified what charges Marvellis would or would not face, or why those decisions had been made.

What I know now about the deal Marvelli got did not come from the State, but from public records I located on my own. The information exists and is accessible. It simply was never given to me.

In that exchange, the structure of Jack's case became impossible to ignore. The witness whose testimony carried the most weight would never be asked to answer for it before a jury. His account would be used but never tested in the same way.

The realization did not come with drama—it came with clarity.

Some truths are not announced when decisions are made. They surface later, when someone else finally asks the questions that you were never invited to ask.

For my own peace of mind, this section documents the forensic evidence that should ordinarily be expected in a murder investigation, but in this case, was not presented in court.

This accounting does not suggest that such evidence was never collected or considered, only that it was not introduced or relied upon in this trial. This accounting is drawn from my own review of the proceedings, including extensive notes taken throughout hearings, motions, and trial. It reflects what had been presented in court rather than what may exist elsewhere.

What follows is not an interpretation, but only an accounting.

Despite testimony describing a shooting inside a residence, no forensic evidence was introduced to establish that Rylee was killed inside that house.

There was no blood pattern analysis presented to support a shooting at the location described. No photographs of the floor where Rylee was allegedly shot were entered into evidence. No reconstruction of the interior of the residence was offered. No forensic examination of the kitchen ceiling was documented or presented to determine the source of the blood reportedly observed there.

No forensic testing was presented to tie Rylee's body to the interior of the house. No timeline was introduced to explain how long his body remained inside the residence, where it was positioned, or how that period was verified.

There was no evidence presented regarding cleanup efforts beyond testimony. No documentation of repairs made to the residence. No contact with the rental company to confirm whether flooring, walls, or fixtures were replaced. No invoices, work orders, or photographic documentation were introduced to corroborate claims that the scene had been altered or remediated.

No luminol testing was discussed. No wall removal was documented. No forensic photographs of the alleged crime scene were shown.

There was no physical evidence introduced establishing when the shooting occurred, how long Rylee's body remained at the location, or how the sequence described in testimony was independently verified.

There was no testimony explaining how Rylee's body was moved from the house to the car. No account of who carried him, who was physically involved, or how that transfer actually occurred. There was no clear explanation of what happened in those moments—no details about contact, no description of what should have been unavoidable physical evidence. Those pieces were never established in court.

No geofencing data was presented to place any defendant at the residence at the time of the alleged shooting. No cell phone location analysis was introduced to establish who was present inside the home, who entered or exited, or when.

Similarly, no geofencing or location data was presented for the location where Rylee's vehicle was set on fire. There was no digital location evidence introduced to place any defendant at the fire scene at the time the vehicle burned.

In a case that relied heavily on digital evidence to establish coordination, communication, and conspiracy, the absence of location data tying individuals to either physical scene was notable.

Yet one defendant was convicted of arson in connection with the destruction of Rylee's vehicle.

That conviction was entered without the presentation of geofencing data placing any individual at the fire scene, without location data establishing presence at the time of the fire, and without digital evidence tying a specific person to the act of ignition.

The charge was sustained without the same location-based proof that might ordinarily be expected in a case built so heavily on digital evidence.

The testimony presented a vivid narrative of a crime scene and its aftermath. It described a shooting inside a residence followed by deliberate efforts to erase it. It suggested planning, intent, and concealment—the kind of scenario that would ordinarily generate extensive physical evidence under even the most routine investigative standards.

No such evidence was introduced.

The absence of forensic evidence does not prove what did or did not happen. It does not establish innocence or guilt.

But it defines the limits of what was demonstrated.

And those limits matter.

Three men had been charged in connection with the investigation into the death of Rylee James Styler: Jack Henry Thomas, Tyler Jacob Lee Chapell, and Marvellis Armon Miller. Each case proceeded differently, and each resolved without a murder conviction.

Jack Henry Thomas was charged with first-degree murder in connection with Rylee's death. He was also charged under the Kansas Racketeer Influenced and Corrupt Organizations (RICO) Act for his alleged role in a coordinated drug distribution enterprise involving alprazolam and related substances.

The jury found Jack Henry Thomas not guilty of first-degree murder. He was, however, found guilty of violating the Kansas RICO Act.

The drug charges were based on the evidence gathered during the course of the investigation into Rylee's death. Those charges resulted in felony convictions in a related case involving the distribution of alprazolam. Although prosecuted separately, those drug convictions arose from the same investigative effort that followed the homicide.

Tyler Jacob Lee Chappell was charged with first-degree murder and violations of the Kansas RICO Act as part of the same investigation.

During Tyler's trial, the court granted a directed verdict on the murder charge, finding that the State failed to present sufficient evidence to allow that charge to proceed to the jury. Tyler was also acquitted of the racketeering charges. His trial resulted in no convictions related to Rylee's death.

As with Jack, evidence uncovered during the investigation into Rylee's death also resulted in separate drug charges against Tyler in an unrelated prosecution. Those charges were resolved independently but stemmed from the same investigative origin.

Marvellis Armon Miller was initially charged with first-degree murder and racketeering violations in connection with Rylee's death.

Marvellis did not proceed to trial on a murder charge. Instead, he entered into a plea agreement and pleaded no contest to amended charges. Those charges included unlawful distribution of marijuana, unlawful distribution of a counterfeit controlled substance, arson, obstructing apprehension or prosecution, interference with law enforcement, and criminal possession of a weapon by a felon.

Marvellis Armon Miller has not been convicted of murder and is not currently charged with murder in connection with Rylee's death.

Jayden, who was referenced during the investigation that began with Rylee's death, was not charged with murder in connection with Rylee's case. Evidence uncovered during that same investigation resulted in separate drug charges against him in an unrelated prosecution. Those charges led to a prison sentence imposed prior to the trials that followed. Jayden did not appear as a defendant in the murder proceedings and did not face trial for Rylee's death.

The tone of the courtroom changed the moment Jack entered.

He was restless and agitated. Not composed like he had been throughout earlier proceedings. Before the hearing began, I heard that he had been acting up while in custody. Whether that was accurate or not, his demeanor that day was unmistakably different.

When the judge spoke, it was clear this would not be a routine proceeding. The judge addressed him firmly. Not yelling, but assertive. Direct. The kind of voice used when control is already slipping.

Jack interrupted almost immediately. He did not want to confer with his attorney. He insisted that the judge proceed with sentencing without delay.

His insistence was not measured. It felt frantic and uncontained. It was as if whatever restraint he had maintained throughout the trial had finally collapsed. He had no visible awareness of the courtroom, the process, or the stakes. Only urgency. Only agitation.

He spoke over the judge. He spoke past his attorney. The formality of the setting seemed irrelevant to him. The composure he had shown in prior hearings was gone.

His anger was unmistakable. Explosive. Unfiltered. It carried no calculation and no performance. It felt raw and uncontrolled, as though he had reached the end of his willingness to cooperate with the process at all.

As I watched, something shifted for me. Not as a conclusion, but as recognition. This was the first time I felt I was seeing him without restraint. Without strategy. Without the version of himself that had been presented throughout the proceedings.

That moment stood in sharp contrast to the version of him the court had been asked to consider throughout the trial. The testimony had described a controlled sequence of events. A calculated narrative. A version of conduct that relied on planning, restraint, and deliberation. Even the defense strategy depended on that composure.

What unfolded at sentencing did not match that picture.

The agitation was not strategic. The anger was not contained. There was no effort to manage impressions or consequences. Whatever control had been present during the evidentiary phase was gone.

It did not prove anything. It did not resolve unanswered questions. But it disrupted the story his attorney had just finished telling the week before.

For the first time, the behavior in front of me aligned with the volatility described in fragments throughout the case but was never fully explored. It was a reminder that trials are built on what can be presented, not necessarily on what exists.

The judge attempted to regain control of the hearing, instructing Jack again that he was required to consult with counsel before sentencing could proceed.

Jack objected loudly. He said the sentence would put him in prison longer than he had been alive.

The judge repeated his instruction.

Jack then announced that he was firing his attorney. He stated that counsel no longer represented him and again demanded to be sentenced immediately.

At that point, the judge called for a recess.

Members of the sheriff's department who had been guarding Jack escorted him out of the courtroom. The room shifted as he left. The tension did not follow him out, but it did not resolve either. It simply settled.

While he was gone, the judge spoke with both sides. The discussion occurred off the record. When proceedings resumed, sentencing was postponed. It was rescheduled for the following week.

I did not return for that hearing.

I felt I had seen enough. Whatever composure had been presented during the trial had fallen away. Whatever restraint had been maintained was gone. I felt I had seen something unmasked that day, something I could not unsee. It felt like watching the devil dance, and I was content not to be present for what came next.

The sentencing proceeded the following week without me.

Jack Henry Thomas was sentenced to 190 months in prison on the racketeering conviction in Rylee's case. That sentence was ordered to run consecutively to a prior sentence of 150 months imposed in a separate drug case that arose from the same investigative thread.

The total term of incarceration imposed on Jack Henry Thomas is 340 months.

That equates to twenty-eight years and four months in prison.

Jack was correct. The sentence exceeded the number of years he had been alive at the time of sentencing.

What followed was an account of outcomes across the remaining cases.

Tyler Jacob Lee Chappell was not convicted of murder or racketeering in connection with Rylee's death.

Evidence uncovered during the investigation that began with Rylee's death led to separate drug charges in an unrelated prosecution. In January 2023, Tyler was sentenced to eighty-eight months in prison for possession with intent to distribute marijuana, possession of drug paraphernalia, and interference with law enforcement.

That equates to seven years and four months in prison.

Marvellis Armon Miller did not proceed to trial on a murder charge. He has not been convicted of murder in connection with Rylee's death.

On October 2, 2024, Marvellis was sentenced to a total of 113 months in prison, with the sentences on each count ordered to run consecutively.

That equates to nine years and five months in prison.

Evidence uncovered during the investigation that began with Rylee's murder also resulted in separate drug charges against Jayden J. Morgan in an unrelated prosecution. He was convicted and sentenced to a term of incarceration of sixty-eight months.

That equates to five years and eight months in prison.

The Ashes That Remain

Chapter Thirteen

Living With the Results

When the trial ended, I understood something that had taken months to surface.

The court had done what courts do. It processed evidence. It applied rules. It reached outcomes that fit within the structure it was designed to operate within. From a procedural standpoint, the case moved forward. Charges were brought. Verdicts were returned. Sentences were imposed.

And yet, nothing about that movement resolved the question that had brought me there.

The trial created a legal record; it did not create understanding.

What unfolded inside the courtroom followed a logic that only made sense within that space. Evidence was introduced where it fit and was excluded where it did not. The story that emerged was shaped not only by what existed but by what could be proven, charged, and sustained under the law. That process did not fail; it functioned exactly as designed.

What I struggled to reconcile with was how far that design could drift from lived reality.

I sat through testimony that felt detailed and hollow at the same time. I watched narratives form without anchors. I listened as events were described with certainty, even when the physical record beneath them was thin or absent. The system did not require completeness, only sufficiency.

What was sufficient for the court was not sufficient for me.

That does not mean the verdicts were wrong. It simply means they were limited.

The trial answered narrow questions. It did not answer the one I carried with me every day. Those two truths did not cancel each other out. They existed side by side, uneasy and unresolved.

For a long time, I believed that if I paid close enough attention, if I followed every motion, every witness, every exhibit, those two truths would eventually converge. That the legal outcome would align with the reality I was trying to understand.

It never did.

Instead, I learned how to hold both at once: the court's version of events and the unanswered weight of everything that remained outside its reach.

That tension did not resolve itself when the trial ended. It simply became quieter.

And that quiet mattered.

Once verdicts were returned and sentences were imposed, the case entered a different phase. The questions that remained were no longer active. The system was no longer required to solve them. There was no mechanism for addressing what had not been proven, only for finalizing what had been.

The silence that followed was procedural. Clean. Complete.

What that silence protected was efficiency. Closure for the court. Finality for the docket. A sense that something had been resolved, even if the resolution addressed only part of what had happened.

What that silence erased was complexity.

There was no space left for uncertainty or contradiction. No space for the parts of the story that could not be neatly charged or sustained. Once the case was over, those parts were no longer relevant to the system.

They did not disappear—they were simply set aside.

Outside the courtroom, there were no follow-up explanations. No acknowledgment of unresolved questions. No reckoning with what the evidence could not establish. The silence did not feel like neglect; it felt like design.

Inside that silence, my role shifted.

I was no longer a participant in an active process. I became someone expected to accept that the process had worked. That justice had been served because movement had occurred.

But movement is not the same as meaning.

Surviving the trial required compartmentalization. There was no other way to sit in that courtroom day after day and remain functional. I learned how to separate roles. I learned how to listen without reacting and to absorb testimony without responding to it as a mother.

Inside the courtroom, I became an observer. I took notes. I tracked testimony. I followed procedure. I learned the language of motions and objections and standards of proof. I focused on what was being said, not on what it meant.

That compartment worked when it had to.

What I did not understand at the time was how far that separation went. I was not just managing emotion—I was dissociating.

I can see it now in my notes. The handwriting that I do not recognize. The styles and spacing that I have never used before or since. The pages that are filled with meticulous detail I have no memory of writing. Entire days documented clearly and accurately, with no corresponding memory of being present for them.

At the time, I told myself this was focus. Discipline. Control.

It was survival.

For a long time, I believed justice would look like answers.

Not perfect answers and not even complete ones. Just enough clarity to understand what had happened and why. Enough accountability to know that what was done to my son had been seen, measured, and named for what it was.

What the process offered instead was movement.

Justice, as it had been applied here, was procedural. It was bounded. It was designed to resolve cases, not to resolve loss.

I came to understand that the court was not trying to answer my questions but its own. Once those questions were satisfied, the process had ended, regardless of what remained unresolved.

That realization did not arrive all at once. It surfaced gradually, through absences, through narrowing focus, through entire lines of inquiry falling away without comment once they no longer served the case that could be won.

This was not a failure of effort; it was a difference in purpose.

The system delivered what it was built to deliver. What it was never built to provide was meaning.

That is what I had to build myself.

Holding both truths at once did not bring peace, but it brought clarity. The kind that does not soothe, but steadies. The kind that allows grief and realism to coexist without demanding resolution where none exists.

Chapter Fourteen

The Reality of Survival

This chapter begins where everything people expect to end.

The trial has passed. The verdict has been delivered. The system has finished speaking. There are no more court dates to circle on a calendar and no more official moments meant to explain what happened. What was supposed to arrive with answers has already moved on.

What remains did not arrive all at once.

It arrived slowly, in the quiet after the courtroom had emptied. In the long drive home. In the ordinary days that followed something that was supposed to feel final and did not. It arrived in the realization that nothing about life returns to normal just because a process concludes.

This chapter is not about evidence, testimony, or outcomes. It is about what continues when those things stop. This is about what lives on after the language of justice has been exhausted. About the weight that stays when there is no longer anything left to wait for.

There is a particular loneliness that comes after a trial. The world assumes closure has occurred. That something has been resolved simply because it was decided. But resolution requires understanding, and understanding was never offered here.

So life resumes without it.

This chapter exists in that space.

It holds the days and years that followed the verdict in June 2024. The decisions that had to be made without guidance. The ways grief shifted once it no longer had a formal place to sit. The quiet work of continuing when the structure that held everything up suddenly disappears.

It is about endurance, not triumph. It is about choosing to remain present without answers. It is about learning that survival is not dramatic, and resilience is not loud.

It is about what stayed standing when everything else had burned.

From here, the story does not move forward neatly. It moves inward. It moves through the costs that remain, the love that persists, the memories that refuse to be reduced to an ending, and the meaning that has to be built instead of given.

This is not an epilogue.

It is what comes after.

I did not choose resilience; circumstance pressed it into me. It was pressed into me by a loss that did not ask permission. By systems that failed quietly. By the responsibility of continuing when stopping was not an option.

There were days that I wanted the easy way out. There were days when continuing felt like punishment, not courage. Days when getting out of bed felt less like strength and more like compliance. I do not say that for effect; I say it because it is true.

I do not want to be mistaken for a hero.

I was angry. Sometimes, at the world. Sometimes, at the system. And sometimes, at Tom. I was angry that he died and left me here as the only parent standing. I was angry that survival was assigned, not chosen.

That anger does not cancel love; it lives beside it.

If there was one thing that made stopping impossible, it was this: too many people were still here. Children who needed a parent who remained. Lives that depended on mine continuing, even when I did not want them to.

So I stayed.

I am rooted here, where everything settled, held in place by responsibility, consequence, and love that did not loosen just because grief demanded it.

Not healed.

Not settled.

Not at peace.

This is where it leaves me.

Awake in a way I was not before. Aware in a way I cannot undo.

And I am no longer carrying the silence.

That silence is visible now. Documented, set down in these pages, where it can no longer pretend it is neutral or harmless. Whatever quiet once surrounded my son's death will be broken again and again each time these words are read.

This book exists because the silence did not deserve to survive me.

People assumed I would drink again. Some of them said it out loud. Most did not. But I could feel it in the way conversations paused, in the careful looks, and in the quiet readiness. As though relapse was not a question of *if,* but of *when.* As if the worst thing imaginable had finally happened, and addiction would naturally reclaim me now.

A few people told me later that they were waiting. They were waiting for the call, waiting for the confession, and waiting to tell me it was okay and to offer comfort in the form of permission.

I never asked for that permission. But it was there.

Visible. Unspoken. Heavy.

The assumption made sense to them. I understood it intellectually. I had already gone down that road once. I had already lost my husband, turned off life support, and been left to raise my children inside a grief I did not know how to survive. Drinking had followed that loss like gravity.

But drinking did not fix anything.

It did not save me then but only delayed the moment I would have to face what had already happened.

So, when my son was murdered, I knew exactly what alcohol would offer me.

Quiet.

And I knew exactly what it would take from me.

Rylee was the line I would not cross.

The last time I saw him in person, I was newly sober. I was fresh out of recovery. He hugged me and smiled, clearly proud of me. Not relieved. Not hopeful. Proud.

That memory outweighed every craving of silence the alcohol would provide.

I would not let my son's death be the reason I drink again. I would not let his memory be diluted by the same thing that has already taken too much from our family.

Whatever happened next, it would not be that.

That does not mean sobriety was easy.

Some days, I wanted to drink desperately. Not to celebrate. Not to escape responsibility. Not to disappear. I wanted to drink because my mind would not stop.

I could hold myself together all day. I could function, parent, work, respond, and speak in complete sentences. I could appear composed. But when night came, and everything went quiet, my thoughts did not.

They circled.

They replayed.

They interrogated me without mercy.

Every decision I had ever made. Every moment I wished I could change. Every version of myself I was afraid I had failed to live up to. Grief, guilt, fear, regret—all of it lined up the moment the lights went out.

Alcohol could, if even only temporarily, make it quiet.

That is the part people do not like to hear, but it is the truth.

It did not make me happy.

It did not make me careless.

It did not make me feel free.

It made the noise stop.

For a few hours, my mind slowed down enough to rest. The questions stopped firing. The self-punishment paused. The constant replay of what I could not fix finally lost momentum.

That silence felt like relief.

I could tear myself apart all day long, and drinking was the only thing that interrupted it. Not solved it. Not healed it. Interrupted it.

There were other reasons, but they mattered less.

It helped me sleep.

It dulled the edge of memory.

It softened the panic that rose when I had no answers.

But none of those was the reason.

The reason was quiet.

And choosing sobriety meant choosing noise.

It meant learning how to sit inside my own head at night without anesthetic. How to survive the hours when no one was watching and nothing demanded my attention except my thoughts. How to feel everything I would have once numbed and still remain standing in the morning.

That work is harder than drinking ever was.

Sobriety was not an act of strength; it was an act of loyalty.

To my children who still needed a mother who remained present.

To myself, even when I did not feel worth protecting.

And most of all, to my son.

I stayed sober not because I was strong, but because I was unwilling to let his death take one more thing from me.

And I will live with the noise.

Because the quiet alcohol offered was never peace.

It was just absence.

People talk about the loss of a sibling as if it is secondary grief. As if it exists in the shadow of parental loss and therefore carries less weight. That assumption could not be further from the truth.

Research shows that sibling loss is associated with increased anxiety, depression, survivor guilt, and long-term disruption to identity and attachment. But statistics cannot capture what it actually feels like to live inside a home where a sibling has been murdered. They do not explain how grief embeds itself into daily life, routines, and relationships, into the way a family moves through ordinary moments that no longer feel ordinary.

I see my Rylee in Sydney. Sometimes in her expressions. Sometimes in the way she laughs or the way she pauses before speaking.

Some days, the resemblance feels grounding. Other days, it is unbearable. It is a reminder that grief does not divide neatly. It overlaps. It echoes.

The four oldest kids—Sydney, Jason, Nathan, and Rylee—shared the same paternal DNA. The same genetic line. The same complicated history. That connection bound them together in ways that do not require explanation but carry weight all the same. When one of them says their brother was murdered, it alters their identity. It reshapes how safety, permanence, and adulthood are understood.

The younger girls carry a different kind of grief, but no less devastating.

Lily, thirteen, carries her grief in motion. She started wrestling when she was five, first because of her dad, and then because of her brother. Wrestling was theirs before it was hers. When I watch her on the mat now, there are moments when I see Rylee in her stance, in the way she moves without hesitation, in the way she refuses to back down. Other days, I hear him in her voice, yelling at her sister to stop looking at her "dawgs." It was the same sharp, half-teasing command Rylee used constantly. It stops me every time.

Logic says grief does not carry DNA. But genetics do not follow logic. Sometimes, they show up in muscle memory, language, and instinct. Watching Lily wrestle is watching the past surface in real time, familiar, undeniable, and impossible to explain away.

Sadie, ten, experiences grief in cycles. Every few months or so, she climbs into my bed missing her Bubba. Not because of a bad dream. Not because something triggered it. Just because the loss resurfaces when her body can no longer hold it down. It is quiet and tender and achingly familiar. It is proof that grief does not leave; it only becomes more tolerable for a while before returning.

Sadie carries pieces of Rylee in ways that catch me off guard. The eye roll, the timing, and the way she says "Bruh" with the same tone he used when he was ten. These moments are not performances or imitations. They are inherited. Unconscious. Another reminder that love and loss travel through families in ways that cannot be reasoned with or neatly contained.

Both girls had already lost their father ten years ago. If you do the math, they were only one and three then. They grew up without a father. And now they are growing up without their brother.

This is the part that is rarely discussed: compounded grief. Loss layered on top of another loss without recovery time in between. These children are learning how to survive absence before they have fully learned what safety feels like. Grief has become part of their development instead of an interruption to it.

Inside our home, the ripple effects never stopped. Sleep disrupted. Anxiety expressed sideways. Emotional regression followed by sudden maturity. Questions that have no answers. Silence settling into spaces where laughter once lived.

In the middle of all of it, I am expected to remain stable.

Even when I am not.

Even when I am unraveling internally, I am still the structure holding everything together. The constant. The anchor. The person who gets up, keeps the routines, attends school meetings, and absorbs emotions that are not my own while barely containing my own.

There is no opting out of that role.

Grief in a family does not distribute evenly. It moves unpredictably. It lands where it lands. When the person carrying the most weight is also the one expected to steady everyone else, the cost compounds quietly.

This is what the trial did not touch.

This is what no verdict could address.

This is what the loss took, not just one life, but the version of a family that existed before everything shattered.

And yet, somehow, we remain.

Not untouched.

Not unchanged.

But still here.

The cost does not stop with my children. It extends to uncles, cousins, extended family, and friends who carry their own version of this loss quietly. Some speak it out loud; some never do. Some show up once and disappear because they do not know how to stay. Others stay forever, bound by a shared before and after.

Homicide is statistically rare. In the United States, only a small fraction of families will ever experience the murder of an immediate family member. Researchers estimate that well under ten percent, closer to a few percent, of families are directly affected by homicide across generations. Most people will never sit in a courtroom waiting to hear how their loved one died. Most will never have to explain to a child what it means when someone in their family is murdered. Most will never carry a loss that comes not only with grief, but with unanswered questions, public records, and silence where accountability should live.

But rarity does not mean isolation.

When it happens, the impact is not contained to one household or one generation. It fractures outward. Family systems shift. Relationships strain or deepen. Holidays change shape. Conversations become careful. Children grow up faster. Adults learn how to carry things they were never meant to.

This is not just our story. It is uncommon, but it is not singular.

About a year after Rylee was killed, something shifted.

The shock had worn off enough for my body to respond to what it had been holding back. The nightmares had started just after the initial thirteen days, but they soon changed. They became more intrusive. More physical. The smell of burning flesh stopped being occasional and became routine.

It was not a memory I could reason with. It did not arrive as a thought but as a sensation. Phantom smells that pulled me out of sleep and followed me into waking hours. I knew exactly what it was because of my background in EMS. I knew where it came from. And I knew there was no way to outrun it.

Living like that made me difficult to be around.

I was irritable and prickly, sharp at the edges in ways I did not recognize in myself. It felt like suppressing something enormous without being able to name it fully. It felt like bracing against pain without knowing where it would break through next. I was functioning, but only barely. Existing in a constant state of vigilance takes a toll that shows up everywhere.

This was not grief that could be talked through.

This was trauma stored in the body.

It was around that time that ketamine therapy entered my field of vision.

I was working in a pharmacy that compounded ketamine at the time. My boss, Lauren, a doctor of Pharmacology, was deeply knowledgeable about its use in trauma and treatment-resistant conditions. She noticed the residual effects the trial had left on me long before I had language for them myself. She did not diagnose me. She also did not push a solution. She described the changes she had observed over time in patients treated with it, often remarkable, but she was not selling me on anything. She had nothing to gain. She simply took the time to explain what the treatment was, how it was being used, and why it might be worth understanding. Without that conversation, I may never have looked into it at all.

I did not approach it as a last resort, and I did not approach it out of desperation. I approached it the way I approach anything medical—carefully, skeptically, and grounded in evidence rather than hope.

Ketamine therapy is not about sedation or escape. In controlled clinical settings, it is used to treat severe depression, PTSD, and treatment-resistant trauma by working directly on the brain's neurotransmitter systems.

Unlike traditional antidepressants that target serotonin over time, ketamine works on the glutamate system. It helps interrupt rigid neural pathways that keep the brain trapped in cycles of fear, hypervigilance, and replay. It allows new connections to form. Not by erasing memory, but by loosening its grip on the nervous system.

It does not make trauma disappear.

It makes it possible to live without being hijacked by it.

I committed to the process fully.

For seven months, I engaged in structured treatment. It was not easy. The treatment required daily check-ins. It did not numb me. In many ways, it required more honesty than anything I had done before.

Slowly, something changed.

The nightmares became less frequent.

The irritability softened.

My nervous system began to stand down, inch by inch.

And then one week passed.

For the first time since Rylee's death, I went seven full days without smelling my son's burning body.

That week mattered more than anything I could explain.

It did not mean I was healed. I still take a ketamine troche (medicated lozenge designed to dissolve slowly in my mouth) every night. It also did not mean the grief was gone. It only meant that my body had learned it could exist without constant threat. It meant I could breathe without bracing. It meant sleep no longer felt like an ambush.

That week is why this book exists at all.

Until then, writing would have been impossible. I could not ask my mind to return to the details while my body was still living inside the fire. Ketamine therapy did not give me answers. It gave me access. Access to memory without being consumed by it. Access to truth without self-destruction.

Only after that did writing become something I could approach instead of survive.

This was not a shortcut—it was a necessary intervention.

This is part of the story, whether it is comfortable or not, because without it, there would be no book.

There are people whose presence altered the shape of this loss simply by refusing to step back.

My brother, Travis, and my new sister-in-law, Rennae, shared their wedding reception weekend, so our family would not have to travel twice. Their decision mattered more than they will ever understand. It allowed space for grief without adding another logistical burden. It allowed people to show up once, fully, instead of splitting themselves in half.

Some from Rylee's biological dad's side did show up when it counted. His Aunt Pam came to the celebration of life in Kansas with three generations of family. In Montana, Ry's great-aunts Bonnie and Karen, his great-uncle Fred, and his wife Val came. Their presence mattered. It mattered that someone showed up and stood in the space where others' absence was loud.

Then there were the people who knew me long before this book existed.

My EMS/LEO family from all agencies showed up in ways only they could. These were people who had known my children since they were small. They had seen Rylee before life hardened him. They understood how quickly systems fail and how little protection they sometimes offer. They refused to let his memory be reduced to paperwork, headlines, or a case number.

This is where Rylee learned early what I had already known: family is not always biological.

My kids grew up in the EMS world just as much as I did. These people saw my son as a whole human long before the system ever saw him as evidence. They understood the weight of what was taken, and they refused to let the narrative erase it.

If I have not named you specifically here, please know this: it is not because your presence was unnoticed. Many people traveled long distances, from Wisconsin to Seattle, and everywhere in between. They offered hugs, silence, food, childcare, logistics, and support without asking for anything in return.

Every person who showed up for me, and for Rylee, at both events matters. None of that is lost on me.

There are people who lived this with me in ways that were never written in any records.

My daughters.

Sydney is grown, but she's still my child. She might have lived this as an adult, but she was still tethered to her mother and her siblings. There was no clear role for her to occupy and no clean way to carry what was happening. Like all of us, she was affected in her own way, navigating loss and instability without a map.

Lily and Sadie were younger. They were too young to understand why adults disappeared into rooms or why certain conversations stopped mid-sentence. Some truths were delayed instead of explained. They understood more than they should have had to and carried it without language. They lived in the space between death and addiction without words for either.

Jason and Nathan experienced it from a distance, but distance does not remove someone from a family. They still check in on me the way sons do, quietly making sure I am standing.

Survival demanded more than I had. What carried me through was not strength alone, but the fact that we kept moving together.

We grew through this side by side, imperfectly and unevenly. But we bonded in ways that did not exist before. I am grateful for my girls. Without them, I do not know if I would have made it through this fire.

And finally, Joe. He came into my life after the worst had already happened.

He did not know my son. He was not part of the years before the murder, the investigation, or the waiting. He entered after the damage had been done, into a life already shaped by loss.

That mattered.

There was no shared history to lean on. No nostalgia to soften what I carried. He met me as I was then—guarded, angry, grieving, and unsure of how much of myself I could afford to give.

I was not easy. I tested the edges. I picked fights that had nothing to do with him. I pulled back without warning. I carried rage that had nowhere to go and fear that I did not yet know how to name.

Joe stays anyway.

Not by fixing anything. Not by pretending those patterns didn't exist. He did not expect me to be healed; he understood that I had to work on myself. He stayed steady without excusing behavior that would have hardened if left unchecked.

He held space while still believing in growth.

Joe loves me through the parts of me that are hardest to live with.

You have read what I heard and what I felt. You have seen some of the images that existed alongside the record.

Two months before Rylee's death, out of the blue, he sent me a song. There was no conversation before it and no explanation after. Just the song.

He said everything that was in his heart without speaking a single word.

I heard him then.

After he was gone, his voice only became louder.

I cry every time I hear it. Not because of what ultimately happened, but because of what it meant when he sent it to me. I hear my son's voice saying what he could not bring himself to say out loud: "Mom, I'm sorry."

It is not a gentle song, nor is it reflective in a soft way. It is raw, defensive, conflicted, and unresolved. A son speaking to his mother from inside choices he knows she would not want for him. A son trying to explain himself without asking for absolution he does not believe he deserves.

The song does not ask for forgiveness; it asks to be understood.

It is about loving your mother while still moving in a world she would never choose for you. It's about knowing you are hurting her while not knowing how to stop. It is about wanting her to see *you*, even when you cannot be what she hoped.

When Rylee sent that song, it was not random. It was not background noise. It was a message he did not have the language, safety, or timing to say directly.

He was not saying goodbye. He was not confessing. He was not asking for permission.

He was saying: *I know this hurts you. I know you don't agree. But I am still your son.*

What gives that moment its weight is not what happened afterward, but what it confirms in hindsight. Even when he was lost and making choices he knew I hated, he still saw me. He still measured himself against my love. He still oriented himself toward me as his moral reference point.

That matters.

The song holds contradictions. Strength and shame. Defiance and longing. Pride and apology. It does not resolve those tensions because Rylee did not get the chance to resolve them either.

That is the truth this book keeps returning to.

He was not a headline. He was not a cautionary tale. He was a twenty-one-year-old kid navigating a world that asked more of him than he knew how to give.

This is where the words stop because this is where certainty ends. The trial did not resolve what happened. The sentences did not answer the why. The system had closed its file.

If you came to this story expecting a solved murder, the ending may feel as incomplete to you as it does to me. I have never said the law did not do its job. What I learned, only through experience, is that a conviction does not always equal justice.

What remains is this: a son who still knew who his mother was to him, even when everything else was falling apart.

That is not closure. But it is truth. Truth is all I have.

The song was "Momma, I'm Sorry" by G Herbo.

Photographs

What comes next are photographs of Rylee, categorized into three purposes for their inclusion in this book.

The first photographs reflect how I would want Rylee remembered if he were ever seen without context or explanation. They show the person we knew and the life that existed beyond these pages.

The next set includes images I believe belong to the record itself. They are not offered to persuade or interpret, only to stand alongside what has already been written.

And, at the end, are the last messages between my son and me. Those are not part of the record. They are simply the last place I can still find him.

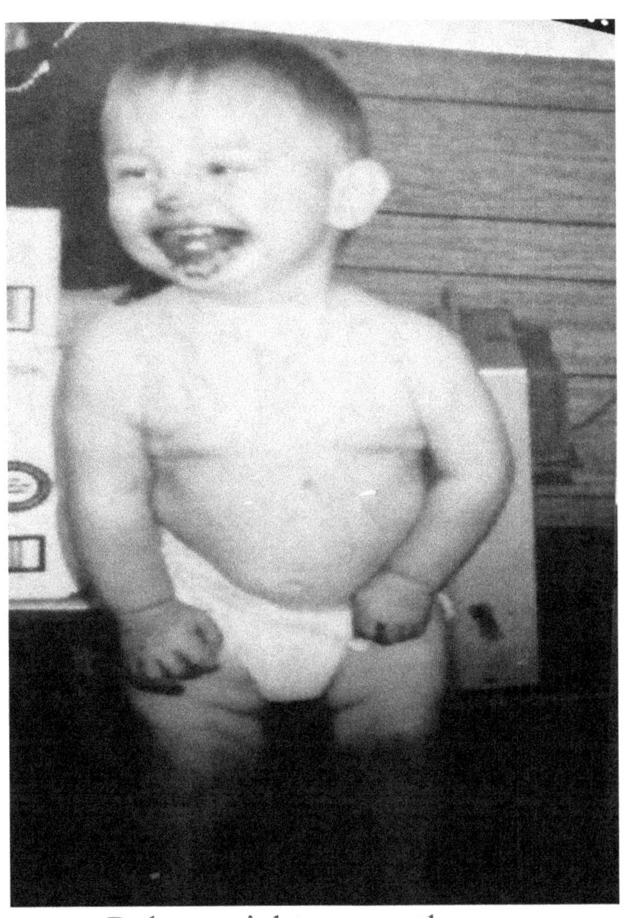

Rylee at eighteen months.

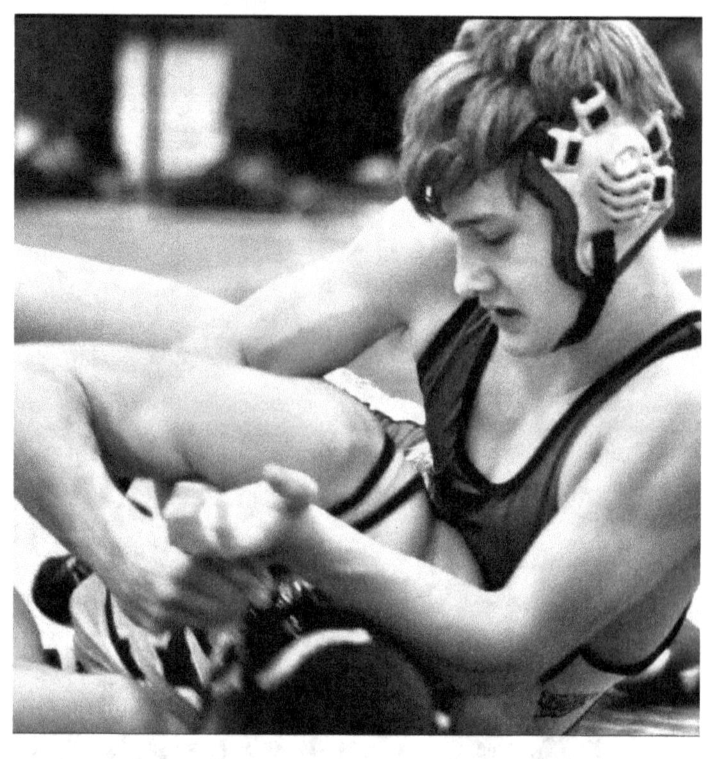

Rylee spent more than half his life on the
mats.

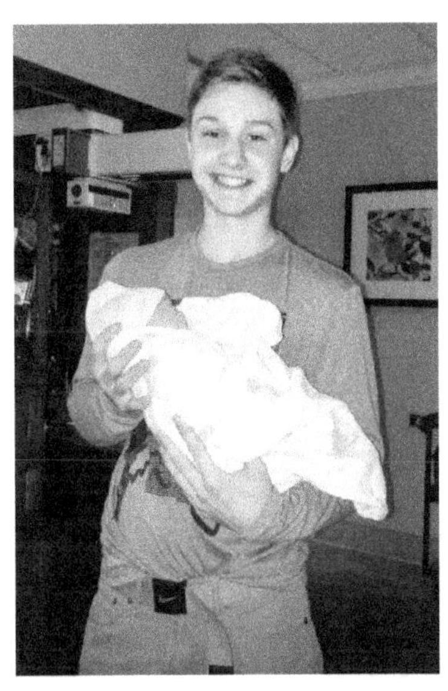

Rylee and Sadie

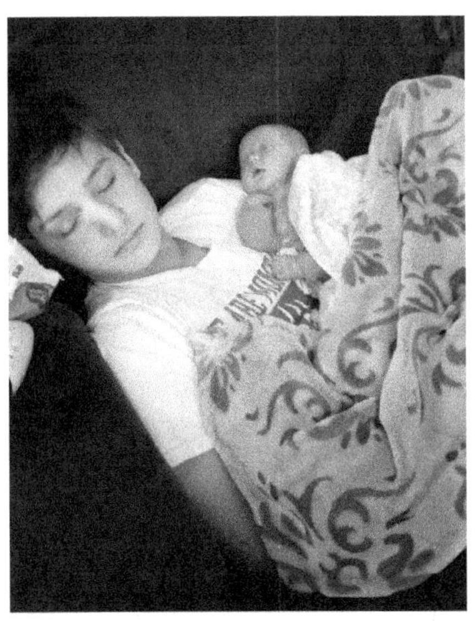

Rylee
and
Sydney

Rylee
And
Lily

Rylee and his dad, Tom

Rylee and Buster

This is how I choose to remember Rylee:
full of life.

Back row L to R: Sadie, Grandma
Merseal, Lily, Myself
Front row L to R: Sydney, Rylee, Uncle-
Travis.
Family has always been important.

The Boys.

The last time I'd ever see Rylee in person:
August 5, 2021

The last video call from Rylee:
Christmas 2021

The Last picture of all the kids together.
Celebration of Life Kansas.
March 2022
(from L to R) Jason, Teri holding Ry, Lily,
Sydney, Sadie, and Nathan

$$ CASH REWARD $$

**IF YOU KNOW
SOMETHING,
SAY SOMETHING**
Up to $2000 Cash
Reward for info leading
to an arrest in this case

Please call (816) 474-TIPS (8477) or scan
the QR code with any information on the
homicide of Rylee J. Styler, whose body was
found inside the trunk of his burning vehicle
the morning of Valentine's Day, 2/14/2022, in
Leavenworth County, KS.

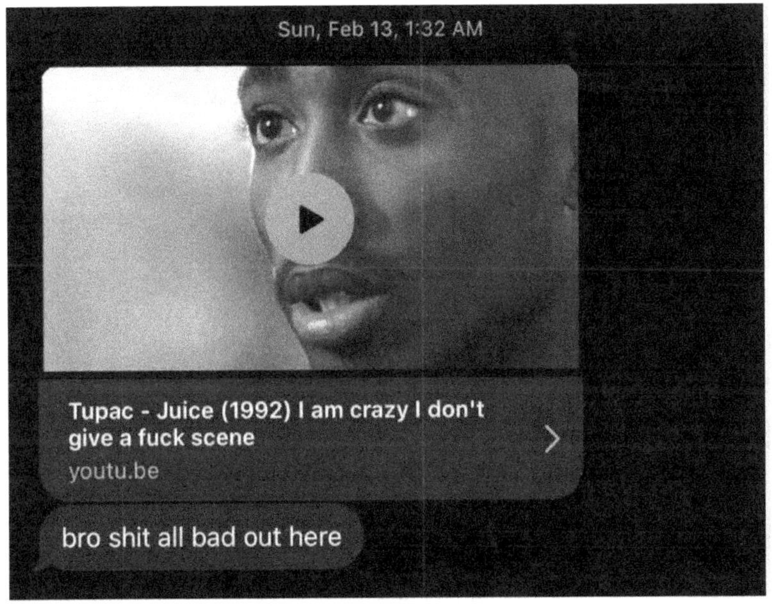

The last messages *ever* sent by Rylee.
"bro shit all bad out here"
Sunday, February 13, 2022, 1:32 a.m.

In *Juice* (1992), Bishop (Tupac) is a symbol of betrayal from within, a reminder that the most devastating harm often comes from those closest, not from enemies.

Hi Teri, I wanted to reach out to you about your son Rylee. I am so very sorry for your loss. My son Dayton use to work Rylee at Home Depot. Dayton has good memories of him.
We actually live off of 195th and Santa Fe Trail less then 400 Ft of where the car was found. I contacted the Sheriff Dept of what our Ring Doorbell captured. Not sure if what was on there was of help. Could see the fire from the video, but not sure if anything else.
Keeping you and your family in our thoughts and prayers

A message worth a million words.

The images transition from darkness to increasing illumination, followed by a brief flash. I do not characterize the event depicted. In motion, it appears as a sudden eruption of light. The location corresponds to where the vehicle was later discovered and is presented in relation to the Ring camera footage of the fire. (400 yards≈133 yards)

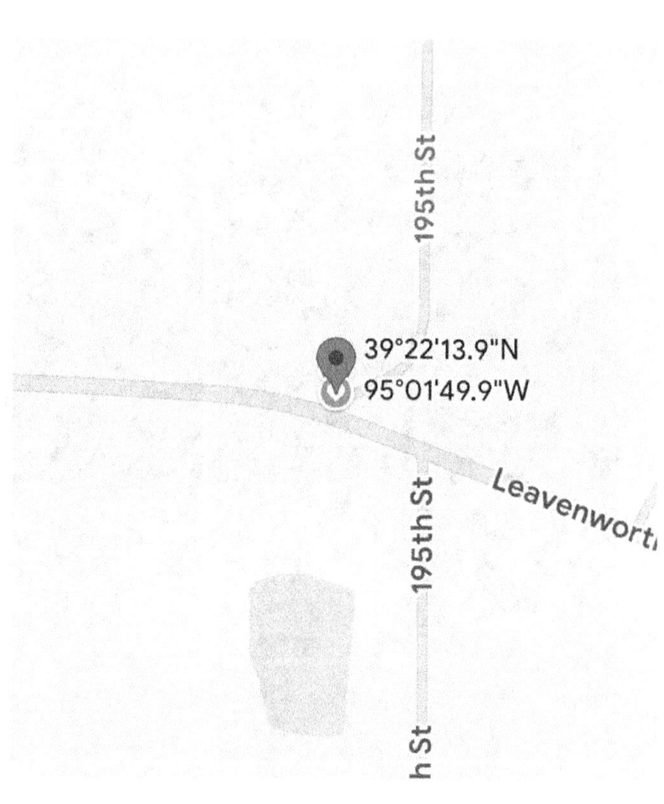

Location of the vehicle fire, and the Cross
I welded.

My first time
welding.

Making the Marker
Cross for
where his body was
discovered.

What follows is the last message from Rylee, and my last messages to him.

To: **Rylee Styles,**　　　　　　　　+

JAN 31, 2022 AT 5:29 PM

Helllloooooo my son!

FEB 1, 2022 AT 9:57 AM

 Hello

FEB 13, 2022 AT 2:28 PM

Hey bubba. Just wanted to check in with you. How's it going??

FEB 14, 2022 AT 3:00 PM

Happy Valentine's Day 

FEB 15, 2022 AT 1:51 PM

 **Audio call**
Tap to call again

To: **Rylee Styles,**

Somehow Leavenworth police got my number and is looking for you " to answer questions about a case" I said I haven't talked to you since Christmas , don't know if your in Missouri or Oklahoma, they asked if I knew an Ashley, I said old girlfriend. I said we don't talk, but I'd give you the message  also said u have no phone I just message you.

913

Jason

Anyways, I definitely don't expect you to call him. But said I'd message you. I just want you to know they are looking for you.

FEB 16, 2022 AT 10:04 AM

To: **Rylee Styles,**

FEB 16, 2022 AT 10:04 AM

Apparently it's about a car. Idk. They wanted to talk to Sydney. I said I wouldn't give them her info. I told them I haven't talked to you since Christmas-ish.

I hope you are ok.

FEB 19, 2022 AT 6:31PM

Hoping you are in jail at the worst... I'm worried bubba. I love you

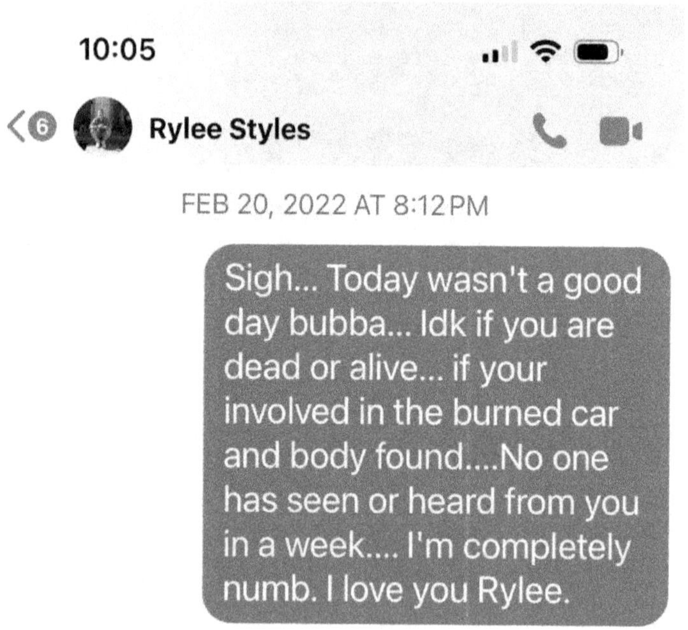

10:05
6 Rylee Styles

FEB 20, 2022 AT 8:12 PM

Sigh... Today wasn't a good day bubba... Idk if you are dead or alive... if your involved in the burned car and body found....No one has seen or heard from you in a week.... I'm completely numb. I love you Rylee.

FEB 21, 2022 AT 4:47 PM

Rylee James Styler

Rylee James was violently taken from us in the early morning of February 14, 2022.

Rylee spent the first half of his life in the 406, as such he developed a lifelong love for the outdoors, fishing, hunting, back country roads and bonfires. In the second half of Rylee's life he embraced life in the 913, where he learned family isn't always blood. Rylee had some fantastic people in his life that he considered his family, he will be forever missed. Anyone who met Rylee knew he had an infectious, goofy smile that lit up any room, day or night. After being the baby of the family to Sydney, Jason, and Nathan, he happily renounced that title to Lily, and Sadie. Rylee was the brother any of his siblings could count on to be there if needed, and was navigating through life to become the man Papa Tom and his Mommah would be proud of. Rylee will always be "Bubba" to his little sisters, and "Ry Guy" to many who loved him. This world will not be as bright without you in it.

Rylee is survived by his Mother (Teri Busse), Siblings Sydney Schmeltz (Austin), Jason Duff, Nathan Duff, Lily Grace Busse, Sadie Lyn Busse, Uncles Travis Eggers (Renee, Maddy) Zack Gardner (Emma and Girls) Aunt Pam Nash (Shane and Girls) Great Aunt Bonnie Bray (Gary and family) and his Biological Dad. Rylee has several other in-laws, out-laws, aunts, uncles, cousins, too many to list, but you are all cherished memories. Rylee was preceded in death by several family members, the closest to him, his maternal grandparents (Dennis and Devera Eggers) Step-Dad Thomas A. Busse Jr (Papa Tom), and Uncle Gary Paul Styler.

In lieu of flowers, please enjoy some of Rylee's favorite things: Family, friends, music and a bonfire.

Celebration of life in Leavenworth Kansas March 26, 2022 2-4 pm
Helden-Larken Funeral Home, 707 S. 6th St. Leavenworth, KS

A Celebration of life for Rylee's Montana family will be June 5, 2022 in Missoula, Time and Location to be announced.

Sent

    Aa  

The 13 days ended.

The silence didn't.

About the Author

For twenty-five years, Teri Busse worked on the front lines of crisis. As a paramedic, she responded to emergencies where life changed in seconds and decisions had to be made without hesitation. Over the years, she also worked in emergency rooms, served in the fire service, and spent time as a corrections officer, experiences that shaped how she understands systems, accountability, and human behavior under stress.

She is pursuing a doctorate in psychology, continuing a lifelong focus on trauma, resilience, and how people survive what should break them.

Teri is the mother of six and lives in Colorado. Her writing is grounded in lived experience and a commitment to telling difficult truths with clarity and honesty.

13 Days of Silence is her account of the murder of her son, Rylee James Styler, and the complicated search for answers that followed.

In his memory, she established the Rylee James Memorial Scholarship for welding, honoring the path he was beginning to build. More information can be found on the *Justice for Rylee James* Facebook page.

Teri also writes under the pen name T.L. Everheart.